I HAVE A NEW NAME

FORGET THE OLD NAMES.
ANSWER TO A NEW CONFIDENCE,
A NEW PURPOSE, & A NEW NAME.

HOSANNA WONG

I HAVE A NEW NAME

All rights reserved. No part of this book may be reproduced or transmitted in any form or by any means, electronic or mechanical, including photocopying and recording, or by any information storage and retrieval system, without prior written permission by the publisher.
Published by Hosanna Wong Ministries, San Francisco, California in partnership with Design Inspirations, Phoenix, Arizona.
Copyright © 2017 Hosanna Wong
All rights reserved.
Design by: Lindsey Pruitt Co.
Photography by: Stefanie Vinsel
Edited by: Stephanie Coats
Printed by: Design Inspirations

ISBN: 978-0-692-90600-2

Scripture quotations marked DRA are taken from the Douay-Rheims 1899 American Edition of the John Murphy Company, Baltimore, Maryland. Accessed on BibleGateway.com.

Scripture quotations marked ESV are taken from The ESV® Bible (The Holy Bible, English Standard Version®). ESV® Permanent Text Edition® (2016). Copyright © 2001 by Crossway, a publishing ministry of Good News Publishers. Used by permission. All rights reserved.
Scripture quotations marked ISV are taken from The Holy Bible: International Standard Version. Release 2.0, Build 2015.02.09. Copyright © 1995-2014 by ISV Foundation. All right reserved internationally. Used by permission of Davidson Press, LLC.

Scripture quotations marked MSG are taken from The Message. Copyright © 1993, 1994, 1995, 1996, 2000, 2001, 2002. Used by permission of NavPress Publishing Group.

Scripture quotations marked NIV are taken from The Holy Bible, New International Version®, NIV® Copyright © 1973, 1978, 1984, 2011 by Biblica, Inc.® Used by permission. All rights reserved worldwide.

Scripture quotations marked NLT are taken from the Holy Bible, New Living Translation, copyright © 1996, 2004, 2007 by Tyndale House Foundation. Used by permission of Tyndale House Publishers, Inc., Carol Stream, Illinois 60188. All rights reserved.

Scripture quotations marked VOICE taken from The Voice™. Copyright © 2008 by Ecclesia Bible Society. Used by permission. All rights reserved.

Printed in the United States of America
2017—First Edition

TO MY HUSBAND —

For your incredible strength and leadership...

For the risk-taking, boundary-pushing, road-paving, all-in, no-turning-back kind of way you love God and fight for His people...

For every moment you have made my heart kinder, my world bigger, and my faith larger...

Thank you.

I love you.

And I love being fearless with you.

FOR PERSONAL USE —

Each chapter concludes with a Questions & Action portion. Sometimes you'll be prompted to grab a pen and paper and complete a short exercise — so have those handy! Sometimes you'll be given goals throughout the week — so get excited! This section is for those who would like to dive deeper into the text.

FOR SMALL GROUP USE —

Each chapter concludes with a Questions & Action portion that can be read aloud and answered by individuals in your small group.

Ideas for leaders: Start your first meeting with introductions (perhaps a snack and an activity) and watching "I Have a New Name" (found at hosannawong.com) on a screen. Afterwards, ask the group how it made them feel, what it made them think of, and what they're looking forward to in reading this book together.

If you're not going through the entire book, read ahead and discover what chapters you'd like to assign for participants to read during the week.

Assign a chapter(s) for the upcoming week. The following meeting, ask the group how they liked the chapter, read the Questions portion aloud — leaving time for as many people to answer as possible — and talk through and participate in the Action portion together. If it requires a pen and paper, have those tools ready for the group.

Reading ahead and choosing which chapters will be best suited for your group allows your study to go for as many or as few weeks as you want, and allows you to assign as many or as few chapters as you see fit. Four weeks would be a typical timeframe, as the first week would be the video and intro to the study, and each following week could cover each of the book's three sections. This could look like assigning participants one chapter of your choosing from each section or multiple/all of the chapters from each section between meetings.

Tailor this book specifically for your group, and find more resources, videos, and small group ideas at **HOSANNAWONG.COM**

TABLE OF CONTENTS

---

i	"I Have a New Name" Spoken Word
01	Intro

PART I – THE ENEMY'S VICTORY ENDS HERE

05	Chapter 1 – Plagiarized
15	Chapter 2 – Soundboards
25	Chapter 3 – The Race
41	Chapter 4 – Fight

PART II – OUR VICTORY BEGINS HERE

53	Chapter 5 – It Is Written
71	Chapter 6 – Childhoods
89	Chapter 7 – Unchained
99	Chapter 8 – Changing Names
111	Chapter 9 – Learning "J"

PART III – GOD'S VICTORY IS HERE

125	Chapter 10 – The Dance
135	Chapter 11 – Figless
145	Chapter 12 – Vintage Boots
155	Chapter 13 – Heaven on Earth
167	Chapter 14 – They Have A New Name
181	Notes
183	Thank You

I HAVE A NEW NAME

SPOKEN WORD PIECE

WATCH VIDEOS OF THE SPOKEN WORD
"I HAVE A NEW NAME," AT **HOSANNAWONG.COM**
OR LISTEN TO THE TRACK ON ITUNES
UNDER THE NAME HOSANNA POETRY.

I HAVE A NEW NAME

SPOKEN WORD PIECE

God spends a lot of time in the Bible

Telling us who we are

It's almost as if He knew that we would doubt

Who that was from time to time

It's as if He saw it coming

That we'd spend our whole lives searching

For what our identity, what our real name was

And that there'd be many moments in our lives

Where we'd let different kinds of names define us

When we've looked in the mirror

Compared ourselves to pictures

And heard the name

Ugly

When we've been left my loved ones

People we trusted once

And heard the name

Unworthy

When we've been drowning in discouragement

Living in a seemingly never-ending crisis

And heard the name

Forgotten

When we've had have our hopes up and our hearts open

Only to be brought down by closed doors

And we've heard **Rejected**

When we look for infinite, affirming love

Through lesser, physical, fleshly versions

When we give it away or when it was stolen

And we hear **Impure**, we hear **Garbage**

When we go to other vices to ease our pain

And we hear **Addict**, we hear **Forever Broken**

When we feel like we've living

In the shadow of someone else's calling

And we hear **Second Place**

When our pain cripples us to a point

where we don't even know how to let others in

And we hear

Lonely

When our past seems too gross for others to forgive

And we hear

Disgusting

It's overwhelming

The voices we're constantly hearing

It's suffocating

This air of constant critique and comparing

And it's sort of *amazing*

The people whose voices I've allowed to name me

The power I've given to my past, to my mirror,

and to my surroundings, and enabled them to

identify me

The amount of years I've spent living up to whatever others say over me

But God says something else about me

It's like He knew there would be other voices

So He wrote His voice down in a timeless

Book of truths that would remind us

Over and over again

In the moments when lies would block His truths

And somehow make us forget

I'm going back to The Source,

not the people who I've allowed to represent God to me

But the actual, literal, tangible words that He has written down for me

And there's some other names He's given to me...

John 15:15 —

He calls me **Friend**.

1 Thessalonians 1:4 —

He calls me **Chosen**.

Ephesians 2:10 —

He calls me His **Workmanship**.

He calls me His **Art**. He calls me **Hand-made**.

He calls me **Purposed & Fashioned** for good things.

1 Corinthians 6:19 —

He calls my body a **Temple**.

He calls it the **Residence** of the Holy Spirit.

Acts 1:8 —

He calls me His **Messenger** to the world.

Galatians 3:26 —

He calls me His **Child**.

Romans 5:8 —

He calls me **Greatly Loved**.

John 8:36 —

He calls me **Free…Free, Indeed**.

2 Corinthians 5:17 —

He calls me **Brand New**.

And it's amazing how different these names are

from the names I'm used to listening to

And in my journey to discover who I really am

In my battle to uncover the truths of myself

I've learned something new about my name

and now this is what I am certain of

My name is not the name the world calls me

My name is not the name my past calls me

My name is not even the name my own mirror calls me

But my name…

My name

is the name

I answer to.

And I can choose today

From this moment forward

To answer to a new name

When I hear, "**Lonely…**"

That's not me.

When I hear, "**Disgusting…**"

That's not me.

When I hear, "**Unworthy…**"

I don't even look over my shoulder.

When I hear, "**Broken...**"

They must have confused me.

Please, look elsewhere.

When I hear, "**Ugly, Abandoned, Useless, Forgotten...**"

I figure someone just has to remind them.

Maybe those were my old names

But they're no longer the names that I respond to

My name is the name I've chosen to spend my days living up to

And if these other voices

Are not saying

The same thing that the Truth is

I look in my mirror and I repeat this:

"They have no right to be speaking to you."

When you stop answering to your old names

They stop having power over you

The names that

My Father

Eternity's Author

The World's Creator has called me

Are the only names that I answer to

When I hear **Friend of God**

That's my name

God's Workmanship

That's my name

Chosen

That's my name

Loved, Wanted, Created with a Purpose

That's my name

God's Temple

That's my name

God's Messenger

That's my name

Free

That's my name

Child of God

You must be looking for me

Greatly Loved

You must be calling for me

Brand New

That is my name.

That is the name that I respond to.

The Enemy has no power here

Perfect Love casts out fear

And Perfect Love has named me and you

What is your new name?

What is stirring up inside of you?

When you hear these words, that His Word,

that The Word has proclaimed

What do you know is the name God is calling you?

Maybe it's not the name you grew up with

Maybe it's not the name your old friends associate you with

Maybe it's not the name that your whole life

you were used to identifying with

But it's the name you now answer to

So when the Enemy tries to get to you

It's the name you introduce yourself with

As for me

My name is **Forgiven**

My name is **Free**

My name is **Brand New**

Loved, Wanted, Child of God, Created with a Purpose

And it's been a *pleasure* to meet you.

I HAVE A NEW NAME

INTRO

Let's get to the point.

Many of us have been answering to some old names for far too long.

Let's just get to the point.

We do not need a book about those memories, past identities, or past names. We already know *those* far too well.

So let's get to the point.

I don't have the time, and you don't have the time— we have wasted enough of our lives answering to our insecurities, answering to our fears, and answering to the limitations other people have put on us. We have wasted *enough* time settling for less.

We want more.

More joy.

More hope.

More purpose.

More confidence in who we are.

And isn't that the point?

Why *don't* we know who that is?

Certainly, people try to tell us all the time.

So why are we still unsure?

What has stood in our way?

Who has stood in our way?

What fears, insecurities, and lies *still* stand in our way?

How did we get here —

This place where, deep inside, we are not sure who we are when we wake up in the morning, and when we go to bed at night?

This place where we ask ourselves questions like—

Who is this person in my mirror?

Do I like them?

Do I trust them?

Do I believe in them?

Why don't we know the answers to these questions?

How can we live a life of confidence, purpose, and joy without *knowing who we are?*

We can't.

We need the answer.

This book was written to help us find it.

The world gives us a lot of names.

God gives us other names.

Together, let's discover what is a lie, what is truth, and claim victory over our lives by answering to a new confidence, a new purpose, and a new name.

The Enemy's victory *ends* here.

Our victory *begins* here.

God's victory *is* here.

And that is the whole point…

PART I —

THE ENEMY'S VICTORY ENDS HERE

CHAPTER 01

PLAGIARIZED

I have answered to a lot of names in my life.

Some I am proud of, and some I am not.

Perhaps you have too.

Perhaps, like me, you've wondered how so many names made their way in, and why so many old names are still a part of you.

It has taken me some time, but I realized the main reason why I have answered to so many of the *wrong* names is that I have spent years not going to the *right* sources.

And I'm not the only one.

Perhaps we each need to re-evaluate where our sources are coming from.

COPY AND PASTE

At some point in school, we were all assigned to write a paper on a book, a play, or a movie. Some of us read the book, went to the theater, or watched the film, and we wrote the essay. Others of us didn't make the time, or have the desire to go through all the hassle, and some of us just didn't care. We just wanted to pass the class.

So how did we get the information to write the paper?

We asked those who *did* read the book. *What did they think of it?*

We read reviews about the play. *What did other people like about it?* We looked online to see what random strangers said about the movie.

Copy and paste a few summaries... done! That's good enough!

We used these other sources to piece together our own paper in hopes of fooling the teacher— and perhaps ourselves—that we had an at least semi-accurate picture of this work... without ever having personally experienced it ourselves.

When we did not have a personal encounter with the source, and instead, portrayed other people's opinions as our own, we plagiarized.

When it comes to piecing together our identity, we are guilty of this same thing.

We ask people around us. *What do you think of me?*

We overhear what others say or listen to gossip. *What do other people like (or not like) about me?*

We look online and read comments, review likes, scan articles, and watch the news to discover what people say about us personally or about our age group, race, social class, interests, and the groups into which we've been categorized. *Copy and paste a few summaries about me... done! That's who I am.*

We are walking around with plagiarized identities.

We are piecing together other people's perspectives, copying and pasting other narratives, portraying others' opinions as our own, and at times are fooling *even ourselves* into thinking we know who we are. Or, at least, that this patchwork version of ourselves is *good enough*.

And yet, we are not personally experiencing The Source ourselves.

We don't know who we are because we are neither reading nor listening to what the original Author of Our Identity—the Creator of Humanity—is saying about us.

While we are looking to other people and other circumstances to define us, the Word of God, an entire book filled with truth after truth about who we are, sits on our shelves, under our beds, and in storage gathering dust. Our freedom is written upon pages unopened, buried by material possessions we're in bondage to.

Maybe some of us don't make the time, or have the desire to go through all the hassle, and maybe some of us just don't care. We're just trying to make it through this life. We don't need an A. We just want to pass, and have at least a semi-accurate picture of ourselves.

In literary and academic worlds, plagiarism is a serious ethical offense. In many sectors, it can constitute copyright infringement, and in many schools throughout the country, after a first or second offense, one could be expelled.

However, the penalty for a plagiarized identity is not expulsion, termination, or any type of legal repercussion. Instead, it's greatest threat is that we could live an entire life that is filled with *far less* than what is available to us.

There is no summary, no hearsay, and no review that can compare with a firsthand encounter with the Original Source.

LIFE ABUNDANT, NO LESS

In John 10:10, Jesus says, **"The thief comes only to steal and kill and destroy. I came that they may have life and have it abundantly."** (ESV)

Ready to get wild? Here are two more translations of this same verse, just to go crazy and have some more fun—

"My purpose is to give them a rich and satisfying life." (NLT)

"I came so they can have real and eternal life, more and better life than they ever dreamed of." (MSG)

Even though these versions translate the phrase differently, the Greek word each one is expressing to us is the same: *perissós.* This word means *greater, excessive, abundant;*[1] *beyond what is anticipated, exceeding expectation; going past the expected limit, more than enough,*[2] *over and above, more than is necessary, and superadded.*[3]

Superadded? I straight up love that word. Who knew that was a real word? It makes me think of choosing toppings for my frozen yogurt, adding an excess of Oreos, cookie dough, granola, and sprinkles (yes, all of that, take your judgement elsewhere), and then—praise be to God—adding *more* on top of it. Excessive, sure. But delicious. Probably holy.

Jesus' *main purpose* was to give us a life that was extremely amazing, over the top and abundant, *superadded*, with all the excess toppings, more than we needed, past all limits, in colors we've never imagined, with joy we've never heard of, and overflowing with confidence, fullness, and exuberant joy that no one else can give us.

Of course the Enemy would want to convince you to have a life that's "good enough."

Of course the Enemy would want you to settle for "just passing."

Of course the Enemy would search through all his best ideas, attempt any strategy he could think of, and brainstorm any plot that could steal, kill, and destroy **anything in your life** that would give you such abundance because *that* abundance is the very thing Jesus came to Earth to give you.

Put simply— every good thing that God wants to give you, the Enemy wants to snatch from you.

KIDNAPPED

Though many translations express John 10:10, and "life abundant" differently, every major translation maintains calling Satan— "the thief." Many of us can attest to how true this title is.

What else refers to a thief?

The word plagiarism comes from the Latin word *plagiarius*, which means *kidnapper*. The word evolved in its Latin meaning to also refer to one who would steal words, as opposed to steal children. The origins of this word always meant that something was being intentionally taken away from its rightful origin, its original maker, and its original purpose.[4]

Our plagiarized identities are *kidnapped* identities.

At one point, we had a home.

At one point, we had safety.

At one point, we knew who we were and where we belonged.

Then the Enemy came to kidnap. He came as a thief. He came with an agenda to steal, kill, and destroy us, to snatch us from safety, from our home, and from our peace. The Enemy came with the *hope* of plagiarism. He threw other sources at us to influence our identity and roadblock us from going to *The* Source— so as to keep our thoughts and ideas of ourselves at "good enough."

He came to keep our names captive, hoping we'd never find our way back to who we are and where we belong— our over-the-top, extravagant, superadded, and excessively amazing home.

CITE YOUR SOURCES

Allowing any other person or any other circumstance to name us is allowing the Enemy—the Thief, the Kidnapper—to abduct us from our rightful origin, our original Maker, and our original purpose.

So who are these other sources?

Let's create a Works Cited page of where we have learned all of our ideas about our identity.

Who are the people we have allowed to define us?

What are the circumstances that we have allowed to determine who we are?

All of the old names that we hear in our heads—when we wake up in the morning, when we look in the mirror, when we go on dates, when we go to work, when we parent our kids, when we go to bed at night— all of those names that tell us who we are—where did they come from?

Who said them?

When did they say them? And why?

What authority do those sources have to name us?

We can so often be plagued with old names, some of which we have answered to for a very long time, but rarely do we take the time to stop, think, and identify where these sources even come from. Yet, we have given them an authority that they have no right to. We have lazily become accustomed to a plagiarized identity. And we are living our lives settling for *less* than what God has for us.

We need to re-evaluate our Works Cited page.

Some sources may have some truth. Others may not. If these sources are not saying the same thing as *The* Source—the Word of God—then they have no right to contribute to our identity.
We will not know what is true, and what is a lie, unless we have a personal experience with the Almighty God, and with His Book of Truths.

It's time to cease and desist in accepting whatever names the world throws at us.

It's time to stop accepting other people's comments, reviews, and opinions, and portraying them as our own.

It's time to personally research our true identity.

It's time to have a real experience with The Source.

We can do more than just pass.

We can do more than get by.

We can do more than copy and paste from illegitimate sources.

We can know who we really are.

We can return back Home.

We can receive what is available to us: a life abundant, *no less*.

QUESTIONS

Why is it sometimes easier to listen to what other people say about us, instead of what God says?

What other sources have you gone to in the past, copying and pasting their opinions, and using them to define yourself?

What is a source that you are currently allowing to define you?

Are you content with the definition it gives you? What do you wish was different?

How often are you going to The Source, the Word of God?

What keeps you from going to The Source more?

How do you think your life would be different if you were more confident in who you are, and more certain of your identity?

ACTION

Throughout the course of this book, we are diving into The Source, exploring the names God gives us, and how we can fully, completely, and boldly answer to a new confidence, a new purpose, and a new name.

First, let's identify these old names, expose how the Enemy has kidnapped us, and cite our sources. Let's create our identity's Works Cited page.

Grab a pen and paper (or write in the margins this book; you do you). Take a quiet moment of reflection inside of yourself and answer these questions honestly.

What are the names you have heard in the past?

What are the sources of these names?

When were these names given to you?

How long have you chosen to answer to these old names?

Based on what you currently think about God, which of these names do you think line up with what God says about you?

Which of these names would you like to stop answering to?

Look at your list. What is this list teaching you? Throughout this book, we are going to take this list, these past sources of your identity, and see if they agree with The Source, the Word of God, and what God is saying about who you are.

THE ENEMY'S VICTORY ENDS HERE.

—

LIFE ABUNDANT,
NO LESS

CHAPTER 02
SOUNDBOARDS

"I Have a New Name" was by far the most difficult piece I have ever memorized.

Memorization is a skill I've worked hard at over the years. Certainly, some pieces are more difficult than others. Some take weeks to memorize, others only days. For the most part, they are all very different, but up until "I Have a New Name," each piece had one thing in common— they all contained stories that I knew really well. It wasn't hard to, at least, memorize the basic concepts and outlines of these pieces because they are all true stories of my life, and I can vividly remember the events. This part of the process can be very natural. The words can feel like a part of me. After all, I've spent most of my life living them.

However, the portion of the piece where I am quoting Scripture— direct names God gives us—made memorizing "I Have a New Name" extremely difficult. I became frustrated trying to remember the references to each verse, the order I placed them in, and what the names even were. It took longer than any portion of any piece ever has. I grew discouraged. I thought about taking the verses out. I thought about scrapping the piece altogether.

Then, I realized why this piece was so much harder.

These verses were not stories I knew really well.

This memorization process was going against what felt natural. These words were not a part of me. I had not spent years of my life living them.

Why can truth be so difficult for us to accept? Why is truth so hard for us to walk in and live by?

We're simply not used to it.

AN UNNATURAL TRUTH

Truth is not painted on billboards along our daily commutes. Truth is not decorating magazines waiting for us in grocery store checkout lines. Truth is not delicately floating amongst our social media, sweetly swimming amidst a sea of kind, loving, and encouraging comments (if someone does want to make a social media platform that is only filled with that kind of positivity, I'll be your first user).

Truth is not the picture we see everywhere we go. Truth is not the sound we hear every day. Truth has become *unnatural* for us to hear.

In a world that only can only benefit from manipulating us—continuously selling us the products they say will solve the problems they've convinced us we have—businesses and media platforms are not going to help us discover what they are strategically trying to hide from us. We are not going to naturally, nonchalantly, accidentally hear truth everywhere we go. We have to fight for it. We have to be strategic in making sure it is a part of our daily routines. We, not the world around us, are solely responsible for normalizing truth in our lives.

The world gains nothing from us knowing our true identity. The only person who benefits from that is us. We are the ones who gain by immersing ourselves in truth. We must be intentional and committed to surrounding ourselves with it—

So that we know these stories really well.

So that they become natural.

So that these words become a part of us.

So that we can spend the rest of our lives living them.

Memorizing the first part of "I Have a New Name" was, in every respect, easy. I'm stating the names that have defined us for so long—names that our pasts have given us, that our surroundings have given us, that our own mirrors and our own insecurities have given us—and those I know really well.

These are names I hear every day. These are names my loved ones hear every day. These are names I hear people say to others, names I see people comment to others, and ones I read painted across the Internet every day. I'm used to these words. I memorized that portion in the blink of an eye.

If we're being honest, many of us, right here and now, could easily recite the names we hear from other people and the world around us. But many of us could not recite the words of God that contradict each and every one of those names.

That is, unless we start getting strategic with the names and voices we surround ourselves with, and what we are choosing to get used to.

VOLUMES

Imagine a giant soundboard, with various knobs and volume controls, each with a label on top of it representing every noise we hear. There's a control for our friends, a control for our Instagram, a control for our teachers, one for our TV shows, and another for our mentors— there's thousands of individual controls, stretching further than our eyes can see.

Now look at the state of your soundboard right now.

What is turned down low?

What is turned up loud?

What are we allowing to resound throughout the speakers of our soul?

Do we know we're in control of what we turn up and what we turn down?

We are the producer of the music of our souls. We choose what we are mixing in. We have authority over the sounds we are getting used to, the tracks that we are playing on repeat. We need to pay attention and constantly re-evaluate the controls on our life's soundboard.

This looks different for everyone; we each have different voices in our lives, and not all of our soundboards have the same controls. For me, I look at how often I'm on the Internet, how much I'm stretching my schedule to go to social events with people who drain me, how many times I check social media, whose opinions I'm caring too much about, and how much time I'm wasting not relaxing *or* being productive. We all know what that means— just being mindless, drowning in pointless noise I'm so used to that sometimes I don't even notice.

Whenever I do not like the voices resounding in my soul, I check back on all of these volume controls. I look at the specific sources of these sounds. I look at the exact culprits of these voices.

If I think, "There's too much noise *there*," I turn that volume down.

I've learned to say, "I don't have to listen to that."

I delete those apps. I cancel those plans. I block the profiles of people that are hurtful. I stop spending time with people who talk down to me. I grab ahold of my social calendar, and I prioritize my time better.

If I look at the controls that speak truth and give me life, and think, "*That's* not loud enough," I turn that volume up.

I've learned the power I have over my own time.

I replace time with the world with time in the Word. I make a plan and I commit to it. I replace pointless social events with meals with people who challenge, encourage, and inspire me. I call my mentors, I call my girlfriends, and I make those conversations happen. I intentionally fill up empty time with things that bring my life joy, and strategically make opportunities for truth to be louder in my world.

Carl Jung, the founder of analytical psychology, once said, "The world will ask you who you are, and if you don't know, the world will tell you."[5]

If we keep allowing volumes of lies, insecurity, and negativity to surround us, at some point we will start to listen to them— and eventually, we might believe them. The names we are listening to will define the names we are answering to. We must be careful of what we allow into our ears, into our eyes, and into our time. Our perspectives, our hearts, and our lives depend on it.

To summarize, here's how to turn down the negative voices in your life:

Step 1 - Decide what you don't want to listen to.
Step 2 - Don't listen to that.

TURNING IT UP

I have spent enough of my lifetime allowing other people to manage what I think of myself and how I live my life. Now, having learned from my mistakes (and still learning), I have spent years practicing adjusting these volume controls.

Now more than ever I am certain—if I am forgetting who I am, what my value is, how I should treat people, or how to have the most out of life—I know exactly what volume, what Voice, has been turned too low for far too long.

It is within our power, discipline, and commitment, to amplify God's truths in our lives. We can do this to the point where it becomes natural and easy to know and recite what He says of us because we know these truths so well. It is our choice to look at our lives' soundboards, and turn His volume up.

"The instructions of the Lord are perfect,
reviving the soul.
The decrees of the Lord are trustworthy,
making wise the simple.
The commandments of the Lord are right,
bringing joy to the heart.
The commands of the Lord are clear,
giving insight for living.
Reverence for the Lord is pure,
lasting forever.
The laws of the Lord are true;
each one is fair.
They are more desirable than gold,
even the finest gold.
They are sweeter than honey,
even honey dripping from the comb."
(Psalm 19:7-10 NLT)

The Word of God is the most freeing, life-giving, world-rocking, truth-speaking volume control we can choose to turn up. The sound waves of these truths *revive the soul*.

By making reading His Word and listening to His truths a conscious, continuous discipline, His volume will become increasingly louder, to the point where we are *naturally* living our days with the constant music of His truths singing around us, in us, and through us.

By indulging in His Word, we are turning up some wondrous, healing, beautiful things:

The truth about who we are and what our value is.
The truth about how we get the most out of life.

The truth about how we should approach people.

The truth about love, about life, about God, what He is like, and all that He is saying.

"Your words all add up to the sum total: Truth."
(Psalm 119:160a MSG)

We can put *these* words against the claims of the world and see what is truth and what is not. We no longer have to wonder. It's simple math. If *their words* don't equal *His Word*, their value is zero.

We naturally check our phones, computers, and televisions, so noise is getting in one way or the other. We must *intentionally* check our Bibles and continuously input God's words into our hearts and our minds, otherwise its volume will be drowned out by what we *are* making louder in our lives.

We are in charge of our volume controls.

If we are struggling with voices of doubt, insecurity, comparison, or fear, it may be because we are not taking the reins of our own soundboard. Perhaps we have forfeited power to someone else. Perhaps we have grown lazy. Perhaps we are settling for a life out of control.

With the world's chaos, opinions, and definitions only getting louder and louder, we cannot afford to *not* take authority over the voices echoing in our lives. We must continuously make sure that no other sound is louder than God's voice, God's Word, and God's truths. If we do not take these matters—our hours and our days—into our own hands and start being strategic with our time and with what we are allowing into our eyes and ears, we will fall victim to what is *naturally* around us— the noise of the world. It's constantly encircling us, like a carousel revolving, unless we choose to move our feet and get off the ride. I'm here to tell you, those voices that are not from God? *You don't have to listen to that.*

We can choose the voices we are checking on, listening to, and allowing in.

We can choose the names we are surrounding ourselves with— the truths we are getting used to, the music we are playing on repeat, the stories we are coming to know really well.

We can choose what we turn up and what we turn down.

We can take back control of our soundboard.

QUESTIONS

What are some of the names you hear, see, and read on a daily or weekly basis, being given to you and to others?

Who are the people giving these names?

Which of these names have you heard or seen for so long, that you are practically used to them, almost numb to them? Why are these names used so frequently?

How do you think the world would be different if truth—the truth about what God says about us and the truth about who God is—was normal to hear and to see? What does that world look like?

When you think of being strategic with turning up the voice of God, what sort of practices and disciplines come to mind?

ACTION

Evaluate your life's soundboard.

With a pen and paper, draw your soundboard. This could look as complex as multiple volume bars or circular knobs lined up on a piece of paper, or as simple as straight lines representing each volume control drawn throughout a page. Draw as many as you can think of, labeling each bar by name, representing the voices that are surrounding you. For example, one bar is for your spouse, one is for your children, one— your teacher, your Instagram, that one girl at school, that one guy on Facebook, that one news channel, that one celebrity, etc.

Label their names or titles as specifically as you can. Once you have finished, think on how loud each one is in your life right now. Take the time to think on each control. Mark on the line how loud it is. (If it helps to make a 1-10 meter, do that, or simply fill in your bar, or mark the line you drew)

Look at your soundboard.

What do you learn from your soundboard?

Are you happy with how loud some voices are, and how quiet others are?

What are specific volume controls that you want to turn down?

What are specific volume controls that you want to turn up?

Using another color pen, or using a different symbol of marking, mark on your volume control where you would like each volume to be.

We control what we listen to. We control what we allow to be mixed into the music of our lives.

What decisions and commitments would it take from you to make these desired volumes a reality?

What is a decision you can make this week in order to turn at least one of these controls up, and one of these controls down?

**THE ENEMY'S VICTORY ENDS WHEN WE
TAKE BACK CONTROL OF OUR SOUNDBOARDS.**

———

HERE'S HOW TO TURN DOWN THE NEGATIVE VOICES IN YOUR LIFE:

STEP 1 –

DECIDE WHAT YOU DON'T WANT TO LISTEN TO.

STEP 2 –

DON'T LISTEN TO THAT.

CHAPTER 03
THE RACE

Isn't it crazy how we can be confident in who we are, defeat multiple obstacles, and then one season, one circumstance, or one person can make us doubt everything we've ever known?

Has that ever been you?

It's certainly been me.

More times than I'd like to admit.

In Galatians chapter 5, Paul speaks to a group of people who have also had a drastic change of heart in regards to their identity and their outlook on life. They knew the truth well, and then all of a sudden, they didn't. Something changed.

In verse 7, Paul addresses them saying, **"You were running a good race. Who cut in on you to keep you from obeying the truth?"** (NIV)

I can see this picture vividly.

A couple of my best friends run marathons, and after each race they describe to me how they trained for it, what the event was like, what the roads were like, and the pivotal moments when they passed someone, or when someone passed them. One of my friends even brought a picture to dinner of her crossing the finish line, just to show the rest of us the face of the person behind her that she'd beaten at the last second (my friend is a really nice person, I promise). For runners, these moments are memorable, and every choice they make on the trail defines how they finish.

And of course, each of my friends have a story of when someone cut into them, tripped them, or pushed them, sometimes completely ruining their race. They can describe those moments in great detail. They remember the setting, the situation, and the emotion that came with it.

We can all imagine this pretty well. This has happened to each of us in our own lives.

We can recount the details of our race, our life's journey, our own road, how we have trained for trials, and the people who have run alongside of us— and we can clearly remember the moment when someone cut into us. We were running just fine! We had our pace all figured out! Then someone stepped into our lane, or ran directly into us, tripping us up, and making us slow down or possibly causing us to stumble to the ground. We could present this picture in great detail to anyone. These moments are difficult to forget.

So who cut into *you*?

Who—while you were running—invaded the steadiness of your direction?

Who was the runner that was just a few lanes over from you, or perhaps not even on your racetrack at all, that came in from nowhere and sidelined you?

Can you imagine this other runner?

Can you envision this situation?

Can you recall a vivid picture?

MY PICTURE IS IN A COATROOM

I remember those who cut into me.

I have a few stories I could share.

I have a picture in a classroom.

I have a picture on a park bench.

A picture in a hospital room and in my childhood living room.

There's a picture in the desert.

A picture in a cafeteria.

And a picture in a backstage green room.

My most recent picture is in a coatroom.

At the time, I was running a good race.

Really good, in fact. My pace was steady, my running shoes fit perfectly, and everyone on the track knew me really well.

It had been years since Jesus revolutionized my life, and I had been set free from a lot of old identities.

I had long since identified my old names, and cited all my old sources.

I had spent a decade taking control of my soundboard, and cutting old voices out.

I was killing it at this race.

Then someone cut into me. And I stopped remembering the truth.

I was at an event with my husband.

I went to the next room to grab my coat, and a man of pastoral leadership, who was from a church I've partnered with a handful of times, physically came onto me. As I was realizing what was happening, I froze. No one had disrespected me this way in a long time.

It had been years.

But somehow this moment felt very familiar.

I was cornered, felt out of control, and as he began to touch me, he spoke of the jobs he could get me, the other ministries he'd like to give my name to, and that he believed in my talent and wanted to help me succeed. I was overcome with shock and could hardly make up words until I finally not-so-eloquently exclaimed, "No, no, no— stop!" and left the room, only to enter a larger room where his wife and kids were eating. The whole family came up to me to say goodbye to me, and I was shaking.

Later that night, we were all taking a group picture, where he was behind me, and in such a large group photo filled with other pastors and leaders laughing, smiling, and squeezing as many of us together as we could, no one could see how he was touching me. I began to tear up. I'm certain that if I saw these group photos, I'd see my face crying, looking scared, small, and embarrassed.

That picture was in a courtyard.

I did not tell my husband for a couple of days. I wanted to be out of the state first because I did not want to confront the man or any of his peers. But my husband knew something was wrong, and, after a while, I opened up to him.

He was beside himself.

And the terror in my face— he had never seen me that way before.

My husband never knew the old Hosanna.

I told him stories as we dated, and my college friends continue to tell him more and more anecdotes as time goes on (thanks, you guys), and some I even share about on stage. But he met me years after Jesus changed my life, and he did not know me when I answered to all the old names.

He didn't know me.

When my high school boyfriend would shove me against walls or in the back seats of cars, forcing himself onto me while I cried, begging him to stop.

He didn't know me.

While I cheated on that high school boyfriend and dated many other guys during that time, trying to get back at him—and all men—with the same tactics he hurt me with.

He didn't know me.

While in college I looked for love in many *other* places— hooking up with strangers at clubs, in back alleys, and in college dorm rooms, strangers with faces some of which I can't remember, and names some of which I never knew.

He didn't know me.

While I was living a two-faced life— living promiscuously *while* performing and preaching on church stages.

He didn't know me.

When I fully surrendered my life to Christ and fought for years to stop answering to names like "Unworthy," "Garbage," "Leftovers," and "Fraud," and the one that stood above them all— "Slut."

The soul work that went into turning from those names and being healed from the shame of my own mistakes, was the hardest thing I've ever had to do.

I'll say that again.

I had spent years feeling abused, battered, disgusting, and stuck in a promiscuous life. The work I had to put into my soul, and my mentality, in order to be rid of the old names I felt *I had earned,* was the hardest thing I've ever had to do.

Sometimes the names we give ourselves—the names we feel our own brokenness has earned—are the hardest names to stop answering to.

Years later, a worship leader meets a spoken word artist while she is on tour and she is confident, she knows her purpose, she loves the Church, she has a lot of great friends, she has a career she is proud of, and she is known for being very intentional with all of the men in her life, especially when it comes to dating. This worship leader marries this woman. He hears stories of her past, but that's not the woman he knows.

Now they are married, and another man touches her. As he listens to his wife's quivering voice and sees the distress on her face, he hears old Hosanna trying to convince new Hosanna, that she is not new at all.

And that's exactly how I felt.

Maybe I wasn't new after all.

Maybe new Hosanna was a lie.

Maybe my marriage and my career was a giant scam and I had pulled the greatest con of all time.
I started to think that perhaps I had fooled everyone into thinking that I

was a new person— but the man who assaulted me knew who I *really* was. This man knew the *real* Hosanna. He had looked at me and seen my *real* name. He found me out. He was merely exposing who I really was. Maybe now everyone would know who I really was too.

PATIOS

Weeks later, I shared this story with a couple that's like second parents to me. I needed help. My marriage had not been the same, as I was hardly speaking to my husband. I was carrying around a lot of shame and still did not know how to process what happened.

We were having breakfast on an outdoor patio in Phoenix, AZ, and I shared this secret with them, tearing up in the midst of a beautiful restaurant, feeling like I was exposing to these two amazing people the fraud that I really was. I told them all the names I had been, and that this man had found me out, and now I didn't know what to do.

They looked at me with all the compassion in the world, and their hearts broke with me.

And yet, the words the husband spoke to me held no pity.

He said, "Hosanna, you have not answered to those names in a long time."

There it was.

He continued, "That man does not know the real you. If he thought he did, he couldn't be more wrong. You have an entirely different life. You're nothing like you used to be. Those names haven't been a part of you in a long time. This is who you really are..."

And they both began to speak truths into my life— the names that I had answered to the past few years, the woman of God I had chosen to be, and the new life that I now had. They listed names of pastors, speakers, and leaders I had worked with for a long time, none of whom had ever disrespected me, and each of whom had always recognized me and treated me as my new name— my real name. There in that restaurant, that couple reminded me of how **new** I really was.

That conversation was the beginning of me being set free from that circumstance.

I hope these truths set you free as well:

You are not your old names. Your identity is the name you choose to answer to.

Those old names exist in old pictures, but they are not the present you are currently living.

Who you were **then** is nowhere near as powerful as who you choose to be **now**.

To this day, whenever an old name resurfaces, I continue to revisit these truths.

That picture was on a patio.

CALLING IT QUITS

That powerful conversation began my journey to freedom, but my inner struggle did not end there. It was not the last lie I heard. And it was not the last old name that resurfaced. Following this event came one of the most heartbreaking and painful years of my career. I was lied to, publicly lied about, taken advantaged of, received mass amounts of hurtful and hateful emails flooding my inboxes, and was accused of horrible things that held no truth to them.

I was *devastated* at the offenses made towards me, both in person and in writing. I was *shocked* by the true colors of people I once trusted and looked up to. People's words began breaking my heart, and slowly eating away at my soul. I felt like ever since that coatroom, I couldn't catch a break. Where were all of these lies coming from?

I was in a dark place.

For the first time ever, I told my husband I was thinking of quitting all together. I talked of other career paths I was considering. I talked of how I didn't know if I could do this one more year.

I had never spoken of quitting before.

He knew I meant it.

TELL ME WHO

During this season, I crossed paths with a good friend. Years ago she and her husband co-founded an incredible ministry that I have had the immense privilege to serve alongside. I look up to this woman a lot. She knew a few of the stories from my year and asked how I was doing. I did not want her pity, so I gave her surface answers.

And even with just those... she looked at me with a shocked face.

She said to me, "I can't believe how discouraged *you* are just because of *those people.*"

WHAT?! Was she *kidding* me? I mean, I expected *some* pity!

She continued, "Who even *are* they?"

She and my friends from Arizona would get along really well.

The truth is that she was not new to discouragement. She had been in leadership for years; she had heard it all. She also knew me, my character, and the obstacles I had already overcome. It was not that she was not sad for me— on the contrary, for months she and her husband checked in on me, sent me flowers and sweet cards, and had been beacons of encouragement during this confusing time. They are two of the most caring people I've ever met. So it's not that she was not compassionate. She was merely **unimpressed** by the source of my discouragement.

That picture was in a parking lot.

A NEW ATTITUDE

I used to read the verse in Galatians about running a good race as if Paul was comforting the readers, stroking their hair, and pitying them. Now, I'm not so sure. As I re-read it, I imagine my friend's shocked face and confused toned, and I begin to understand it with an entirely different attitude.

"You were running a good race. Wait... *Who* cut in on you to keep you from obeying the truth? Who even *are* these people?"

We were killing it! Who on earth cut into *us*?

We are not new to discouragement! How are *we* so discouraged by *this*?

We have been running this race for a long time! Who could have *possibly* brought us down?

In this passage in Galatians, Paul answers in verse 8, **"It certainly isn't God, for he is the one who called you to freedom."** (NLT)

It. Certainly. Isn't. God.

Wait it's who?

Oh let's be clear— not God!

The MSG version puts it this way: **"This detour doesn't come from the One who called you into the race in the first place."**

One more version for fun! The VOICE translation says it like this: **"I know for certain the pressure isn't coming from God. He keeps calling you *to the truth*."**

My friend already knew what I came to know shortly after.

Those people were nowhere near powerful enough to name **me**.

I was giving them power that they did not have.

The detour they put my life on did not come from the One who called me to this race *in the first place*.

THE OTHER RUNNER

Not only do our detours of discouragement not come from God, but many times they don't even come from people who are running their own race well. Sometimes those who have cut into us are struggling with their own run.

My friend told me of a time this happened to her during a marathon.

Here is her picture— She had worked hard to train, was gliding along in the fast lane, and everything was going smoothly when a woman directly in front of her abruptly stopped to bend down and tie her shoe, and my friend completely crashed into her.

This other runner was not prepared for this race— she had not tied her running shoes well. She didn't know the rules—or wasn't abiding by them—as to where to pull over when you stop or slow down. And she was not paying attention to the other runners around her— a big no-no for marathon runners. And yet, *this* woman was the person who made my prepared and hard-working friend crash to the ground.

When I think of all the times someone cut into me while I was running a good race— rarely were those people secure in who they were, acting in love, treating me with kindness, speaking to me in a Godly way, or seemed to be running their race as best as they could.

Many of those people were like the runner in my friend's marathon— not well-equipped, did not know better, or simply were not aware of (or did not care for) the other people and other factors surrounding them.

Many people who have spoken discouragement over us or have treated us poorly have acted out of brokenness in their own lives. Many times, when people try to make us feel insecure, they are speaking out of their own insecurities. Many of the names we have heard in the past have come from people who don't even know *their own name*.

Why are we looking to people who don't even know who *they* are?

We must not glorify or be discouraged by runners who still don't know how to run well themselves. They are not God. We read in Galatians that if the detour we are on is not leading to more freedom, then it absolutely did not come from God. We can know for **certain**, He calls us only to the **truth**.

If these other runners were running their own race well, they would not have cut into us in the first place.

The source of all of this discouragement is simply unimpressive.

FINISH

From one runner to another—

I'm so sorry for every moment that someone cut into you.

I'm angry at the moments old names have resurfaced in you.

I'm sorry for your coatrooms.

But more than anything, I am alongside of you, asking you to join me in getting back in this race.

At the end of Paul's life, he writes in 2 Timothy 4:7, **"This is the only race worth running. I've run hard right to the finish, believed all the way."** (MSG)

It's time to get up from this place of defeat.

It's time to start answering to the One who called us here to begin with.

It's time to answer to freedom. It is time to answer only to truth.

It's time to take the power away from this detour. Away from this coatroom. Away from these emails. Away from the people who hurt you. Away from the people who ran into you. Away from the name-callers. Away from the accusers. Away from the people **who don't know you**.

Who are these people? They are now your past. They are not your present. They are not your future. And they are not who called you here in the first place.

The choice of what you answer to is **yours**.

The choice of who you let define you is **yours**.

This race is yours.

Not theirs.

Remember *this* picture.

This can be the moment you start running the only race worth running again.

QUESTIONS

When was a point in your life when you were running a good race? Think on a time you were proud of yourself.

What are some successes you have had in your life? List all or some that have been significant to you. Think about the time you got good grades, the time you got married, the points you made in a basketball game, or the promotions you've received.

Who are some people who have cut into you? Perhaps they stole your joy, hurt your feelings, lied to you, falsely accused you, or abandoned you. Who were *those people*?

Did they make you slow down, or completely fall down? What was the effect of them cutting into you?

How long did it stop you from running a good race?

How did them cutting into you change your perspective or your life?

Have you ever had a time in your life when you had to get up after someone cut into you?

What did it take to get back up, and press onward?

If you have not yet got back up, what do you think it would take for you to do so?

ACTION

Recall the picture of who, when, and where this person, or these people cut into you.

Think on the details.

Grab a pen and paper.

If you are a lover of pictures, draw a symbol representing something from that moment.

If you are a lover of words, write a description of something representing that moment.

For example, if someone spoke hurtful words to you in a classroom, you could draw the windows from that room, or write out what was said to you. You could even take it a step further, if you're a painter, or a songwriter, or express through another medium, and you wish to elaborate more. If not, at least doodle a picture, or write out your pictures in sentences:

A picture in a car.

A picture at a park.

The goal is to identify the moment(s) and draw the picture of when someone cut in.

Now look around you in this moment.

For a runner, every choice they make on the trail defines how they finish. Every turning point remains a memory.

Draw a symbol representing this moment, your surroundings, or perhaps how you feel. For example, if you're sitting in a coffee shop, you can draw the coffee mug sitting beside you, or write about the smells of the coffee brewing, or what this chapter is bringing to your mind.

The goal is to identify *this* moment.

What does the picture of your soul look like right now? What are your surroundings at this time?

If you decide you want to keep running, I encourage you to keep reading. And remember *this picture* of the choice you're making on this journey. If you already made the decision to keep running, draw the picture of *that* moment— those moments of victory.

You can also write out your pictures of victory in sentences:

A picture in a backyard.

A picture on a hike.

Take a moment to embrace, mourn, and celebrate these two different types of pictures.

The Enemy's victory ends when we realize
And mourn the stories of those who cut
Into us, and recognize how unworthy they
Were to do so.

The Enemy's victory ends when we live in the
Knowledge that we are not our past names—
We are who we choose to be.

THE ENEMY'S VICTORY ENDS WHEN WE CHOOSE TO GET BACK UP AND CONTINUE THIS RACE.

> "MY NAME IS THE NAME I ANSWER TO."

CHAPTER 04
FIGHT

I did not get out of my identity funk by people's pity.

It had been weeks since I first talked to my husband about quitting, and I still had not told any of my friends, family, or pastors about the severity of my discouraged heart. I was sitting on my couch reading, wallowing in my sadness and feeling bad for myself, when I got a phone call from a friend. She said she was speaking at a conference in Indonesia, contracted a virus, and while she was sick in her hospital bed, God put it on her heart to call me.

She said, "I have no idea what is happening in your soul. But I am calling to tell you, you can't just sit on your couch and wait for God to heal you. Everyone is discouraged right now. There is a real battle going on. You are going to have to *fight*."

Great. Just more friends with no pity. *Taking applications for new friends immediately.*

But she was right.

I was not fighting at all.

I was upset at the state of my soul, and I was upset at God for allowing such heartbreak to happen to me.

"I do not deserve this," I thought. *"I shouldn't have to fight anymore."*

In her inspiring and challenging book, *Without Rival*, Lisa Bevere writes, "Trials have the power to transform us from who we are into who we long to be. But along the way we picked up the lie that we could be heroes without ever engaging in a battle."[6]

That was me.

I expected to be a hero because of what I had overcome in the past. I expected to be a hero because of how good of a person I was deep inside. I expected to be a hero... without getting off my couch and engaging in battle.

As my friend and I hung up the phone, it was like a blindfold had fallen off of my eyes. *Of course* I could not sit around and wait for my identity to suddenly, magically come back to me. The Enemy had fought long, hard, and *smart* to take it away, I was going to have to get up, strategize, and *fight* to take it *back*.

I am not alone.

There is a battle for each of our lives and each of our identities. The Enemy is constantly fighting for our names and fighting for our lives, and many of us have been sitting on our couches, waiting for our new confidence, our new purpose, and our new name to suddenly appear out of thin air. Many of us are tired of fighting, or have never fought at all. For some of us, we like to pretend that the war isn't happening. For others of us, the Enemy is winning simply because we have forfeited the battle.

TUG O' WAR

Imagine your name—your identity—as a tug o' war rope.

I remember playing this game when I was little, and the sight was something fierce. There were two teams— one on each side of the rope, both calling over other people to help them pull, both digging their feet deep in the mud, screaming chants, sweating their heads off, and cutting their fingers against the rope slipping back and forth until they bled. They fought relentlessly, until one was victorious.

The fight for our names is far fiercer than this.

Let's call it what it is. The Enemy is on one side, and God is on the other. They are pulling with all their might. They are digging their feet in the mud, their fingers are holding so tight they are bleeding, they are shouting at the top of their lungs, calling out different names to us, and passionately warring over our identity.

They are fighting relentlessly, both desperate to be victorious.

Imagine your rope.

What are the ways the Enemy has fought for you?

What are the names he has constantly shouted at you?

Who has he called to be a part of his team?

Now imagine the other team.

What are the ways God has fought for you?

What are the names He is constantly calling you?

Who has He called to be a part of His team?

THE BATTLE CONTINUES

For many of us, the war for our lives is not a simple game. The scoring is not clear-cut. It is not a shutout. It is not even the best out of three. Instead, our whole lives have been spent being tugged between these two teams. We may answer to a new name, but then an old name tugs back. We may be far on the Enemy's side, but then God's group of fighters grabs us. We are then in His territory for years and years, and all of a sudden— the Enemy brings in new team members with new ideas and the war rages on. It is a never-ending battle. Frankly, it is exhausting. *Of course* we are tempted to forfeit.

God, however, is not.

In 1 Corinthians 1:10, Paul is speaking of trusting God and the power of prayer, and he writes, **"He has delivered us from such a deadly peril, and he will deliver us again. On him we have set our hope that he will continue to deliver us."** (NIV)

We see a picture of a God that does not pull once— not twice, but again and again, *continuing* to fight for us.

I love how it's translated in the MSG version: **"… He did it, rescued us from certain doom. And he'll do it again, rescuing us as many times as we need rescuing."**

I love that. He will rescue us as many times as we need. He will keep digging His feet in mud. He will continuously call new members to His team. And He is not tired of fighting. No matter how much we may have given up, He has not.

No battle intimidates God. No downfall scares Him away.

Whenever you feel that you have failed too many times, have used all His grace up, or feel unworthy of His time, know this: **God is excited to hear from you again. Forgive you again. Carry you again. He's not as tired of you as you are of you. Come back again.**

We are His favorite thing.

We are His main job and all of His hobbies.

There's nothing He'd rather do today, tomorrow, or the next day than fight for us, strengthen us, and rescue us again and again and again.

OUR FIGHT

God is fighting. But are we?

We are not talking about fighting to earn God's love, or fighting for salvation. Ephesians 2:8-9 debunks that idea clearly, saying, **"For it's by God's grace that you have been saved. You receive it through faith. It was not our plan or our effort. It is God's gift, *pure and simple.* You didn't earn it, not one of us did, so don't go around bragging *that you must have done something amazing.*"** (VOICE)

So, fighting for God's grace is not even a question. *Pure and simple.* We don't have to fight for that.

What we are talking about fighting for is our perspectives, our self-worth, our identities, our names, our ideas of God and the world around us. We cannot be victorious by being indifferent. We cannot be triumphant while being a lifeless rope. We cannot be heroes without engaging in battle. We cannot have lives we are proud of without fighting for them.

Fighting is a choice that demands *action*.

No more pity. How are we going to fight?

GEAR UP

Let's talk about gearing up.

In Ephesians 6:13-18, Paul writes of the methods we should use to protect ourselves from the Enemy and the methods in which to fight. First, he speaks of our protection:

"Be prepared. You're up against far more than you can handle on your own. Take all the help you can get, every weapon God has issued, so that when it's all over but the shouting you'll still be on your feet. Truth, righteousness, peace, faith, and salvation are more than words. Learn how to apply them. You'll need them throughout your life."

Paul starts with teaching how to gear up for defense— gear up with truth, righteousness, peace, faith, and with confidence in our salvation. In some translations of the Bible, these powerful defenses are referred to as the "Armor of God."

Then he speaks of our two weapons.

"God's Word is an indispensable weapon. In the same way, prayer is essential in this ongoing warfare. Pray hard and long. Pray for your brothers and sisters. Keep your eyes open. Keep each other's spirits up so that no one falls behind or drops out." (MSG)

He tells us how to fight: with the Word of God and prayer.

He says that God's Word is **"an indispensable weapon"** and that prayer is essential for our **"ongoing warfare."**

The war continues. It will not stop during this life.

So.

Are we immersed in The Word?

Are we warring with prayer?

Are we active on this battlefield?

Do we even have the gear?

TEAM UP

If we are going to fight, we are also going to need to surround ourselves with a great team.

One of the biggest mistakes I made during the beginning of that painful season was that I didn't tell my closest friends what was going on. I did not let them into my war, allowing them to fight for me.

Of course I wasn't winning the game. I had benched my best players.

Of course the Enemy was closing in. I did not recruit more of God's warriors to pull on my rope.

Galatians 6:2 says, **"Share each other's burdens, and in this way obey the law of Christ."** (NLT)

The Bible says that it is obedient to share the load— it's His desire for us to carry things together. And yet, I robbed that opportunity from my friends. I robbed those weeks of my life from victory.

More time than I'd like to admit had passed before I fully opened up to my friends, called my mentors, and starting telling the truth about my heart. But I am so glad that I finally did. As my husband, my friends on the patio, my friend in the parking lot, my friend who called me as I sat on my couch, and many other friends throughout the country came alongside of me and fought for me, I realized so much of what I was missing. They had the strength I was lacking. They had the perspective I was missing. They were in the Word and in prayer even when I wasn't. And the only way to win this battle was to embrace this team, start adding more players to this team, and stop going through this battle alone.

We can so often be upset at God for not winning our battles for us, while He's given us the gear and the team to be victorious, and we're simply choosing to ignore it.

THIS IS WAR

I hate the idea that the Enemy could have victory over my life and over my identity. It makes me angry. *No way* am I allowing him to have any joy over my thoughts and decisions. I can't believe the small victories I've already allowed him to have, and the power I've given to so many other names. That time is over. I have now declared war.

During this story, I was not as geared up or as teamed up as I should have been, and, quite frankly, I had stopped fighting. But after my friend called me out on my apathy, all of that quickly changed. Taking care of my soul went from being a passive vacation, to an active daily decision. I doubled my time using my gear— in the Word, in worship, and in prayer. And I doubled my time with my team. First, with my husband. That was huge. We had lots of date nights. We made a commitment to go to the beach together at least once a week for the rest of the year, no matter how crazy work got, and we stuck to that. I became more intentional with friends. I had more team huddles. I made time in my schedule even when it seemed there wasn't any. I was more proactive with being in touch with pastors and mentors in my life, and continued to bring these hurts into the light. Just as Lisa Bevere had written, this trial had the power to transform me into who I longed to be— if I fought for it.

The war was on.

By *actively engaging* in battle, my soul was coming back to life.

I was not allowing the Enemy to win by default.

I was not going to forfeit.

Don't you forfeit either.

The Enemy has had victory over our names with our self-pity, our entitlement to sadness, and our apathy for *far too long*.

Today, I am still fighting.

I am still warring.

Please, join me. Together, let's gear up, team up, and fight for our identity.

QUESTIONS

Imagine your life—your identity—as a tug o' war rope. What lies has the Enemy fought for you with?

What truths has God fought for you with?

Imagine the people on each side of this rope.

In your life, who has the Enemy used to pull for his team?

Who has God used to pull for His team?

In the battle for your identity, have you been fighting, forfeiting, or pretending as if the war isn't happening? How have you been doing that?

What gets in the way of you spending more time in the Word of God?

What gets in the way of you spending more time in prayer— talking to God, saying loving things to God, sharing your feelings with God, asking God for these you'd like, praying for people you love, or praying for people you are struggling to love?

What gets in the way of you confiding in and embracing a good team?

ACTION

For you specifically, with your schedule, and your day-to-day life, what is a realistic practice you can commit to in order to fight for your identity?

How can you fight with the Word of God? How can you fight through warring in prayer?

Think in specifics.

For example, think on if you're a morning or evening person. Think on extra minutes where you are waiting for your children in the car. Think on any type of school or work commute where you could play the Bible on audiobook, or listen to a sermon on a podcast. Think on a free period at school.

Be honest about where you can make room in your life to be reading or listening to the truths found in God's Word, and where you can carve out more time to be intentional spending time with Him.

How can you fight by surrounding yourself with more of your friends who speak life into you?

Think in specifics.

For example, think on how you would have to budget to see friends who are out of town. Think on spots around your neighborhood where you and your local friends can meet. Think on books or devotionals you could do with your friends to be in community and in the Word together over the phone. Think of weekly, monthly, or yearly traditions you could start with these relationships.

Be honest about what it would take to commit to these practices—perhaps a new Bible or a Bible with a certain aesthetic. Perhaps new headphones to listen to the Word on audiobook. Perhaps a couple new plants to put in a corner of your house that you'd like to pray at each morning. Perhaps new fishing rods or a new camera that would be fun to use with your friends when you visit them.

If so, get that cool-looking Bible, buy those nice headphones, purchase all the plants, get your favorite rods and that sweet new camera. Think on what it would honestly take and when you could honestly create that time.

The smallest actions speak louder than the greatest intentions.

Only you know what will work for you and what will help you keep to this commitment. Take an honest second to figure out what those things are.

Write that down.

Choose to commit to it.

This is your battle plan.

Talk to God about your commitment, and ask Him to remind you of it, and help you keep it.

THE ENEMY'S VICTORY ENDS WHEN WE MAKE THE COMMITMENT TO FIGHT.

AND WHEN WE DO... OUR VICTORY BEGINS.

PART II —

OUR VICTORY BEGINS HERE

CHAPTER 05
IT IS WRITTEN

Indeed, *God spends a lot of time in the Bible telling us who we are...*

And that's a very good thing. Because from the beginning of humanity, the Enemy has tried to make us doubt just that.

Satan knows this: There is power in our identity.

In his captivating book, *People of the Second Chance*, Mike Foster says:

"Identity is the engine that drives the relationship not only with ourselves but also with God and others. If your identity is broken, your life is broken. If you define it incorrectly, you will carry that wrong definition into your story. If all you see are your limitations, you will miss out on the stunning possibilities God is creating in front of you."[7]

So it is no surprise that the very first time we see Satan, he is attempting to take this engine—this very important essence of our lives—away from us.

VICTORY LOST

"The serpent was the shrewdest of all the wild animals the Lord God had made. One day he asked the woman, 'Did God really say you must not eat the fruit from any of the trees in the garden?'

'Of course we may eat fruit from the trees in the garden,' the woman replied. 'It's only the fruit from the tree in the middle of the garden that we are not allowed to eat. God said, "You must not eat it or even touch it; if you do, you will die."'

'You won't die!' the serpent replied to the woman. 'God knows that your eyes will be opened as soon as you eat it, and you will be like

God, knowing both good and evil.'

The woman was convinced. She saw that the tree was beautiful and its fruit looked delicious, and she wanted the wisdom it would give her." (Genesis 3: 1-6a NLT)

Satan fought for Eve with a powerful tactic— doubt.

Satan asks Eve, "Did God really say...?" Sneakily trying to make her second-guess what God told her, he even skews God's words ever so slightly from what God originally said, changing the command from not eating from the *one* tree, to not eating from *any* tree. How conniving! Some of the greatest lies in our lives are truths the Enemy has just slightly skewed.

Let us pay very close attention to this: the very first thing Satan says to mankind is "Did God really say that?" The basis of Satan's entire strategy for the victory over our lives is in undermining the words of God, and making us doubt their power and authority. **Satan wanted Eve to doubt God's words.**

In the MSG version, Satan's rebuttal is written, **"You won't die. God knows that the moment you eat from that tree, you'll see what's really going on."** He accuses God of lying, and of hiding truth and goodness from Eve. **Satan wanted Eve to doubt God's intentions.**

He continues to say that *once she eats the fruit* and her eyes are opened, she **"will be just like God, knowing everything, ranging all the way from good to evil."** He implies that God created her faulty, that she was not created whole, that she was not enough, *but* that if she did something—if she ate the fruit—then she would be. He wants her to believe that her actions could make her more important than how she was originally made. **Satan wanted Eve to doubt her value, doubt her worth, and doubt her identity.**

He convinced her. She ate the fruit.

And now here we are.

Let's be honest. We are not too different from Eve.

Satan does not have to shout hateful lies at us or masterfully convince us of extreme falsehoods. He merely needs to quietly make us doubt God, question His intentions, and feel as though we are possibly not enough. Then perhaps, we will go to that fruit—or that *other thing*—to find our worth and our identity in that. "Anything other than God." – that is Satan's whole plan.

Doubt has crept into each of our lives.

We have doubted God's words. "Did God *really* say I am His child? Did God *really* say I am greatly loved? Did God *really* say I am free?"

We have doubted God's intentions. "Why would God do this to me? Does God even want good things for me? What is God hiding from me?"

We have doubted our own worth— convinced that we are not worthy of God, not worthy of our dreams, not worthy of love or joy, and not **good enough** unless we *do something* to make us valuable.

Satan is victorious when we doubt God's words, doubt God's intentions, and doubt our identity.

It's a good thing, then, that God spends a lot of time in the Bible telling us who we are...

VICTORY FOUND

Thousands of years later, we see Jesus in the desert.

He shows us how to be victorious over the schemes of the Enemy.

"Then Jesus was led by the Spirit into the wilderness to be tempted by the devil. After fasting forty days and forty nights, he was hungry. The tempter came to him and said, **'If you are the Son of God, tell these stones to become bread.'**
Jesus answered, 'It is written: "Man shall not live on bread alone, but on every word that comes from the mouth of God."'

Then the devil took him to the holy city and had him stand on the highest point of the temple. 'If you are the Son of God,' he said, 'throw yourself down. For it is written: "He will command his angels concerning you, and they will lift you up in their hands, so that you will not strike your foot against a stone."'
Jesus answered him, 'It is also written: "Do not put the Lord your God to the test."'

Again, the devil took him to a very high mountain and showed him all the kingdoms of the world and their splendor. 'All this I will give you,' he said, 'if you will bow down and worship me.'
Jesus said to him, 'Away from me, Satan! For it is written: **"Worship the Lord your God, and serve him only."'**

Then the devil left him, and angels came and attended him." (Matthew 4:1-11 NIV)

Satan used the same strategies in the desert to try and take down Jesus Christ, the One who came to redeem what humanity had lost, that he had used in the Garden to take down humanity. He tried to make Jesus doubt God's words. He tried to make Jesus doubt God's intentions with those words. He tried to convince Jesus that *if He did something*—if He bowed to Satan—that action would increase His value. And with every doubt Satan tried to instill, he began with the question of His identity: "If you are the Son of God…"

Satan reveals what his greatest threat is— children of God knowing who they are.

But Jesus did not come to play.

When Satan came at Him with lies, manipulation, and coercion, Jesus came back at him with Deuteronomy 8:3, 6:16, and 6:13.

Jesus combats what the Enemy said with what the Scriptures say.

Jesus combats what was spoken with what is written.

Jesus combats Satan's tactics of doubt with what He knows is certain.

THAT'S MY NAME

In both the garden and in the desert, Satan *knew* the words of God and tried to skew their meaning to manipulate the children of God.

He will do the same with us.

We must not allow the Enemy to know more about our identity, our purpose, and our destiny than we do.

When the Enemy attempts to find us alone, unarmed, and without volumes of truth loudly singing around us, and tries to make us doubt what God said, what his intentions are, and what our identity is, we must know God's words so deep in our hearts that we can boldly declare against his lies: **It is written.**

Let's unpack what the Bible says about our identity—what is *written* about those who have chosen Jesus—and choose today to answer to a name that is God-breathed, unchanging, certain, and sure. All of the following verses are either Jesus himself speaking to His disciples, a disciple or apostle speaking to a church or group of believers, or a poet speaking directly to God.

Behold, the Word of God.

When we feel like an outsider—

It is written:

Jesus says, **"I don't call you servants any longer; servants don't know what the master is doing, but I have told you everything the Father has said to Me. I call you friends."** (John 15:15 VOICE)

We are not left alone here on Earth, unaware. The secret to an amazing life is not hiding behind closed doors. We have been let into the wonderful mystery. Slaves may not know what masters are doing. But friends are in it together. Friends support each other. Friends sacrifice for each other. Friends are dependable. Friends ride or die through thick and thin. Friends have your back.

Friend of God.

That's my name.

When we feel like an after-thought—

It is written:

Paul says to the church in Thessalonica, **"to you who belong to God the Father and the Lord Jesus Christ... We know, dear brothers and sisters,** that God loves you and has chosen you to be his own people." (I Thessalonians 1:1, 4 NLT)

The MSG translation says, **"It is clear to us, friends, that God not only loves you very much but also has put his hand on you for something special."**

We are not mistakes. We are not Plan B. We are not God's little afterthought, solely where we are because someone was fired, someone quit, someone died, or someone made a mistake.

Continued in verse 5a: **"When the Message we preached came to you, it wasn't just words. Something happened in you. The Holy Spirit put steel in your convictions."** (MSG)

No matter the physical circumstances that led us to this moment, each of us has the opportunity to allow the Word of God to change us, for Jesus Christ to be the center of our lives, and for the Holy Spirit to "put steel" in our convictions, giving us full and complete confidence in this— God has put His hand on His people for *something special*. When we allow God in, we allow something unique to happen within and through us.

Chosen.

That's my name.

When we feel like our lives are unattractive—

It is written:

 "...**We are his workmanship** (Ephesians 2:10 KJV)," "**We are God's masterpiece** (NLT)," and "**We are the product of His hand, heaven's poetry etched on lives, created in the Anointed, Jesus, to accomplish the good works God arranged long ago.**" (VOICE)

 "**I will offer You my grateful heart, for I am Your unique creation, filled with wonder and awe. You have approached even the smallest details with excellence; Your works are wonderful; I carry this knowledge deep within my soul.**" (Psalm 139:14 VOICE)

We are the handiwork of the Artist of the Heavens and the Earth. When artists create something, they are intentional with the details. Painters pick a certain brush for a certain canvas. Poets pick a certain structure for a certain story. Dancers pick a certain move for a certain song. Photographers pick a certain light for a certain composition.

Artists are detailed, choosey, and take their time to create work they are proud of. So much more is God's intentionality with us. God has approached our details. God has added certain colors. God has played certain songs. God doesn't create second-rate craftsmanship. We are no knock-off brand. We are God's masterpiece. Hand-made. Purposed. And fashioned for good things.

God's workmanship.

That's my name.

When we are ashamed of our bodies, what we have done with them, or what has been done to them—

It is written:

"Don't you know that your body is the temple of the Holy Spirit who comes from God and dwells inside of you? You do not own yourself." (1 Corinthians 6:19 VOICE)

No matter who touched us, no matter who misused us, no matter who took advantage of us, when we look in the mirror, we can say, "I look good today! I'm the place where God's Spirit lives!"

Continued in verse 20: **"You have been purchased at a great price, so use your body to bring glory to God!"** (VOICE)

Our bodies are not for sale. Our bodies are not for display. Our sexuality is not something to be put on exhibit. The Spirit of God lives in us, so we present our bodies as if we are presenting the Temple of God. This body is beautiful. This body is sacred. This body brings glory to God. This Temple is breathtaking— and yet, it's nowhere near as wonderful as what lives inside.

God's Temple.

That's my name.

When we think it's someone else's job to share about Jesus—

It is written:

"But you will receive power when the Holy Spirit comes upon you. And you will be my witnesses, telling people about me everywhere— in Jerusalem, throughout Judea, in Samaria, and to the ends of the earth." (Acts 1:8 NLT)

"So we are now representatives of the Anointed One, the Liberating King; God has given us a charge to carry through our lives—urging all people on behalf of the Anointed to become reconciled to the Creator God." (2 Corinthians 5:20 VOICE)

"Therefore, as you go, disciple people in all nations, baptizing them in the name of the Father, and the Son, and the Holy Spirit, teaching them to obey everything that I've commanded you…" (Matthew 28:19-20a ISV)

Some of us have a story and testimony of God's goodness in our lives that we have *yet* to share. Perhaps we think it is humble to stay hidden? To pretend like our stories don't matter? I have never understood that. That is so weird.

It is *prideful* to think your story is your own and *selfish* to hoard it inside of you.

We are God's Plan A to bring light to a dark world. We are the witnesses, the representatives, the messengers of Jesus. As we go—wherever we're going, whatever we're doing, while we are living our lives—we are to be sharing our story and the story of a Risen Savior, *as if* people's lives depend on it.

Be selfless. Stop holding the hope of the world inside of you.

God's Messenger.

That's my name.

When we feel like our childhood has been stolen—

It is written:

"For you are all children of God through faith in Christ Jesus." (Galatians 3:26 NLT)

"…Whoever did want him, who believed he was who he claimed and would do what he said, He made to be their true selves, their child-of-God selves." (John 1:12 MSG)

If we have been living as anything other than God's children, we have been living all wrong. The VOICE translation says we have **"the right to be *reborn* as children of God."** (John 1:12b)

The moment we choose Jesus, we get an entirely new life, and we get to begin an entirely new childhood. God is not like our earthly fathers. This love and this family is beyond any human limitation. Our true self is nothing other than our child-of-God selves. We can live as who we *really* are— as God's children that He loves and enjoys.

Child of God.

That's my name.

When we feel unloved, unworthy, and so sinful and dirty that we can never be redeemed—

It is written.

"But think about this: while we were wasting our lives in sin, God revealed His powerful love to us in a tangible display—the Anointed One died for us." (Romans 5:8 VOICE)

"Greater love has no one than this, that someone lay down his life for his friends." (John 15:13 ESV)

We are **so loved** that even *while* we were apathetic towards Him, God chose us. *While* we were wasting our lives in sin, He had such a crazy-amazing, wildly-huge, undeniable, undefeatable, never-quitting, never-ending, over-the-top, and excessively extravagant love for us that He laid down his life for us.

He died so we would never have to pay the consequences of our shortcomings. He died so we may have an abundant and superadded life. No one gets an inheritance or the benefits of a will until someone dies. He died for us so we could have it all. He died for us so that when He rose, we could rise from our graves too— our graves of sin, our graves of sadness, our graves of brokenness. He died so we could personally know Him, and enjoy life with Him on this side of Eternity and the next.

In 1st century BC, Publilius Syrus wrote: "Something is only worth what someone is willing to pay for it."[8] That's how valuable, significant, and loved we are. We are worth what Jesus was willing to pay. With His own life, Jesus has declared our worth.

Greatly Loved.

That's my name.

When we feel like we'll never be set free from who we were, what we've done, or how we used to live—

It is written:

"...If the Son sets you free, you will be free indeed." (John 8:36 NIV)

"For when we died with Christ we were set free from the power of sin. And since we died with Christ, we know we will also live with him." (Romans 6:7-8 NLT)

In choosing Jesus to be the King of our hearts and the Lord of our lives, we are choosing a life completely set free from every sin, forgiven for every mistake, and liberated from every chain that has held ever us captive. Period. Through Jesus, the power of sin is dead and gone.

Free Indeed.

That's my name.

When we feel like we are stuck with our old names and our old life—

It is written:

"...Anyone who belongs to Christ has become a new person. The old life is gone; a new life has begun!" (1 Corinthians 5:17 NLT)

If we belong to Christ, everything is new. We are not our old ways. We are not our addictions. We are not our past mentalities. We are not our past mistakes. We are not our old names. Through Jesus we receive a brand new beginning. We are a completely new person with an entirely new life.

Brand New.

That's my name.

Our name is the name we choose to answer to. What is the name proclaimed by the Word of God that you need to declare today?

AN IDENTITY RESEARCHED

The Bible is *filled* with truths about who we are. For some of us, we don't know all these truths yet. We haven't read that many verses. This is new for us. And that's okay! That's to be expected. It was new for Jesus too. By the time Satan approached Him in the desert, He knew the Scriptures well. But He didn't start there.

Philippians 2:6-7 tells us about Jesus that **"though He was in the form of God, He chose not to cling to equality with God; He poured Himself out to fill a vessel brand new; a servant in form and a man indeed. The very likeness of humanity…"** (VOICE)

Jesus gave up His privilege as an all-knowing God, and came to earth as a baby. We know this about babies— they don't know much. Their knowledge starts as a blank page. Just like us, Jesus had to learn who He was.

Though we know much about Jesus' birth and infancy and Jesus' adult ministry, we don't know much of the in-between. However, there is one story recorded during Jesus' childhood. We meet Him in Jerusalem at 12 years old. His family attended the Festival of the Passover and on their way home, they realized Jesus wasn't with the group of people they were traveling with.

"The next day they found him in the Temple seated among the teachers, listening to them and asking questions. The teachers were all quite taken with him, impressed with the sharpness of his answers. But his parents were not impressed; they were upset and hurt. His mother said, 'Young man, why have you done this to us? Your father and I have been half out of our minds looking for you.' He said, 'Why were you looking for me? Didn't you know that I had to be here, dealing with the things of my Father?'" (Luke 2:46-50a MSG)

Here we get a picture of a young Savior, asking religious leaders questions and listening to their answers. We can imagine our Redeemer at 12 years old investigating the Scriptures and all of the knowledge of the teachers in the Temple in Jerusalem. Just like any human child, we see Jesus researching who He is.

In its commentary on verse 49, The Voice Bible points outs that **"as Jesus enters young adulthood, He begins manifesting an** extraordinary sense of identity... He isn't just 'Mary's boy' or 'Joseph's stepson.' He has a direct relationship with God as His Father, and He knows His life will follow a path of working for God."

From this one story of Jesus' childhood, we see He was curious to know more of His history, and we see Him identify himself as God's child.

We too have the opportunity to start from scratch, research who we are, surround ourselves with mentors, teachers, and pastors, ask questions, listen to answers, investigate the Scriptures, and begin our journey of learning who we are. Today is a great day to start.

AN IDENTITY CONFIRMED

There is no record of God speaking directly to Jesus until after He is baptized.

"As soon as Jesus was baptized, he went up out of the water. At that moment heaven was opened, and he saw the Spirit of God descending like a dove and alighting on him. And a voice from heaven said, "This is my Son, whom I love; with him I am well pleased." (Matthew 3:16-17 NIV)

The first time we hear Jesus speak, He is speaking of His identity.

The first time we hear God speak about Jesus, He is confirming His identity.

"This is my Son, whom I love; with him I am well pleased."

Guess what the next verse is?

"Then Jesus was led by the Spirit into the wilderness to be tempted by the devil..." (Matthew 4:1)

Now we are at the scene of Jesus in the desert.

Right after God confirms who Jesus is, we have our first record of Satan talking to Jesus: **"If you are the Son of God..."**

Wow.

We are fighting to know who we are. God is fighting to confirm who we are. Satan is fighting to make us *doubt* who we are.

The fight for our identity: It was at the center of the garden. It was at the center of the desert. It's at the center of the battle for our lives right now.

Because of Jesus, we have an example of how to fight against the schemes of the Enemy and how to claim our identity with boldness, confidence, and steel in our conviction.

Our victory begins when we shut down the lies of the Enemy with the truths we know in the Word of God.

LIKE A STONE

I love this verse in Isaiah 50:7:

**"Because the Sovereign Lord helps me,
I will not be disgraced.
Therefore, I have set my face like a stone,
determined to do his will.
And I know that I will not be put to shame."** (NLT)

The VOICE translation says, **"I set my face like a rock, confident that I will not be ashamed."**

That's the kind of boldness I want.

That's the kind of attitude I want to approach the Enemy with.

That's the face I hope he sees when he tries to come after my identity.

Satan can keep telling those lies. We're done listening to them.

Satan can keep selling us doubt. We're done buying it.

Satan can keep trying to disgrace us, make us insecure, and make us hide.

We will not be ashamed. We will not be brought down.

We have set our faces like stones. We are determined to do God's will.

We are convinced of God's words. We are certain and sure of what is written. We are confident in the names we are answering to.

When the Enemy throws questions at us with his powerful tactic of doubt— we can answer Him with the powerful tactic of confidence. Confidence in who we are. Confidence in what is written in the Word. Confidence in the name we are answering to.

Bye, Satan. It is written.

Sincerely, New Name with Face Like a Stone.

QUESTIONS

When you read the stories of Satan tempting Eve and Satan tempting Jesus, what similarities and differences do you see? What is a main take-away for you?

With these stories in mind, what are times in your life when you have been more like Eve and times when you have been more like Jesus?

When you read the verse Isaiah 50:7, what part sticks out to you?

**"Because the Sovereign Lord helps me,
I will not be disgraced.
Therefore, I have set my face like a stone,
determined to do his will.
And I know that I will not be put to shame."**

What words or attitudes in this verse represent something you'd like to embody?

ACTION

God spends a lot of time in the Bible telling us who we are. It is within our power to spend a lot of time living out those names.

Out of the verses and names written in this chapter, what name do you feel stirring inside of you?

What name do you feel you haven't answered to yet, but you want to start? What name do you want to declare: **"That's my name"**?

Highlight/underline those names and the truths that stood out to you in the words of God that were written in this chapter. Mark this chapter up if need be with circles, lines, and giant letters signifying what your new name is.

If you hate marking up books, write those names down on another piece

The goal is to identify and declare the name(s) that God has given you that stood out to you as your new name.

Here are two goals for you this week. Within the next 7 days:

1 – Each morning you wake up this week, before getting out of bed, say your new name(s). For example: "Good morning, Lord. I am your Workmanship," or "Today, I am Free Indeed." Even if you whisper it— declare it over yourself and over your day. Begin your day with this attitude of certainty and confidence.

2 – Share your new name with someone. This can be as discreet as you calling a friend or writing an email, saying you want to share this new identity with them— or this identity you hope to be more confident in.

As we know, share, and declare the words of God, we begin to live in and live out His words in our day-to-day lives.

OUR VICTORY BEGINS HERE.

—

OUR VICTORY
BEGINS WHEN
WE SHUT DOWN
THE LIES
OF THE ENEMY
WITH THE TRUTHS
WE KNOW
IN THE
WORD OF GOD.

CHAPTER 06
CHILDHOODS

Our victory begins when we start answering to the right names.

What names from the Word of God have been a struggle for you to answer to?

What names have been the most difficult to comprehend?

Without a doubt, "Child of God" has been the hardest name for me to understand, accept, and live by.

LIKE A CHILD

What does it mean to be a child?

To lounge around in grassy fields and just enjoy the sunshine?

To be free of the weights of responsibility?

To be reckless? To be risky? To be curious?

To play with your friends all the time?

To just be joyful and have fun everyday?

To not be constantly anxious about the future or always worrying about the burdens of the world?

To care only about enjoying and laughing and resting, leaving all the cares of the world to the adults?

That wasn't my childhood.

My whole childhood felt like a rush to grow up.

My parents were missionaries on the streets of San Francisco. They planted a church in the heart of the city, catered and committed to reaching society's outcasts— drug addicts, convicts, prostitutes, pimps, murderers, thieves, and homeless on the streets of downtown. We held full services 2-3 times a week, the city's outcasts became our family, and I saw hundreds of people come to Jesus and turn their lives around every week of my childhood. That's how I was raised; those streets were my playground.

Growing up in this environment, my siblings and I saw a lot of things that I didn't realize were out of the ordinary until I was an adult.

I was nine and my brother was three the first time we saw someone murdered in front of us. It was a violent hate crime, and we were the key eyewitnesses to this brutal and grotesque act of bigotry.

That was the *first* murder I saw.

Later that year was the first time a woman attempted to abduct me. As she ran off with me in her arms, I screamed and kicked as our homeless friends ran to my aid and brought me back to my family.

I was 11 the first time I saw my mother assaulted. A man who was pretending to have no movement in his legs jumped out of his wheelchair, laughing and gloating that he was fooling us, and attacked her. He ran away after people began to race towards him.

The next year I was 12, and that was the first time I saw my dad get beat up. A man had walked up to the stage and asked if he could whisper something to my dad while he was preaching. As my dad leaned in, the man grabbed his collar and pulled him off the stage, punching him in the face and gut until he was bleeding all over the floor.

The police and the paramedics arrived, and a volunteer—a college student who was visiting us on a missions trip with her school—offered to walk me around the block, hoping to perhaps distract and comfort me. I'll never forget what she said to me that day.

We walked around the block and she told me to stop crying, and that this is what real ministry takes. Looking back, who on earth let this random woman be alone with this poor little girl after such a horrifying event? She told me that I have to be strong, to not let anyone see me cry, and that living your life for God means living a life of sacrifice, pain, and hardships. There was no reason to worry, she said, because "once we get to Heaven, there won't be any suffering. We just have to wait until then. God wants you to be mature. God wants you to be strong. Don't you want to show God you love Him?"

So I wiped my tears. I put a on a brave face. We headed back to our church, and I watched as my dad walked back onto the stage with bandages and all, and preached his heart out. It was truly incredible. I'll never forget it. Not a dry eye in the house.

I remember that 73 people came to the altar to give their lives to Jesus that day. I remember because I told myself over and over as I battled nightmares the following weeks: "It's worth all this pain. I have to toughen up. 73 people who needed healing gave their lives to Jesus. 73... 73..."

73.

That's a lot of people.

But I was 12. And I needed some healing in my life too.

I didn't feel free to share with my family how scary that moment was for me or how hard any of the things we saw the years before or the years after were. I thought my silent pain was the cost of living a life for God. As far as I was concerned, God wanted me to be mature, be strong, prove my love, and stop acting like such a child.

A NEW PERSPECTIVE

At the time, my family and I all struggled with this same mentality in our own way and on our own. Month after month, whenever something scary would happen on the streets, whenever fights would break out, gunshots would fire, or threats were made against us, we never talked about it. We never dealt with it. We never skipped a beat. A family mantra was, "People are dying every day without Jesus; we're going to tell them about Him no matter what it takes."

Wipe tears. Brave face. *Love God better, Hosanna, get it together.*

I have to be clear— my parents are incredible humans and their tenacity to see souls saved is one of the most amazing things they ever taught me. I knew my whole life that we couldn't be ashamed of the Gospel— a message that could set any captive free. I knew my whole life that our words, our love, and our lives were how God was going to reach a broken world, and we needed to be faithful— that it was a **privilege** to be His hands and feet. I knew my whole life that serving Jesus was hardcore and not always easy, but that people were worth it.

I can never repay my parents for all the wonderful and powerful life lessons they taught me that I still hold tight to. It's why I am so passionate about truth. It's why I'm so certain of the Word of God. I can talk all day about how we need to evangelize our communities better. I can preach all day about how we need to be more passionate in sharing the love of Jesus. I have my parents to thank for ingraining within me a blatant fearlessness in sharing the Gospel.

Later in life, all of us, my parents included, realized that though we had built a ministry we were incredibly proud of, we had not left enough room to be a family outside of ministry— *to enjoy, to laugh, and to rest*. Yes, people needed Jesus and we needed to tell them— no question there. But we also needed to take care of each other and our own souls in the process. After all, Jesus came to give us an abundant life too. How did we miss that? We have since opened up, and healed up, and God has mended our broken pieces and our skewed perceptions of Him so beautifully, bringing each of us much closer together. When my parents started our church, they were newly saved, jumped right into high-capacity, full-time missions work, and I believe that though they were great *parents*, they too were learning how to be *children* of God. In a way, we were all figuring out our childhoods together.

When I think about being a child, I have to sort through some things I was raised believing. It's taken me a while to discover what it means to be a *child of God*. It's taken me a while to figure out what's even allowed.

What exactly are the rules?

How much fun can I have?

CHILD OF GOD

In the book of Galatians, the Apostle Paul speaks to some of the early churches in a region called Galatia. They were preaching that salvation comes from legalistic works and Old Testament laws and many were living enslaved to ceremonial practices, thinking these religious acts would equal eternal life. Paul writes to explain how Jesus changes everything. In chapter 4, he breaks down how free we are because Christ came, died, and was raised from the dead, and the difference between being a slave (how we used to live) and a child (how we can live now, through faith in Jesus).

In 4:4-7, he writes:

"…When the right time came, God sent his Son, born of a woman, subject to the law. God sent him to buy freedom for us who were slaves to the law, so that he could adopt us as his very own children. And because we are his children, God has sent the Spirit of his Son into our hearts, prompting us to call out, 'Abba, Father.' Now you are no longer a slave but God's own child. And since you are his child, God has made you his heir." (NLT)

I resonate with the people of Galatia. They were not in a mental place too different from where I was a few years ago. I was living like I was a slave to a check list, hoping that would put me in good standing with God, and thinking that was the best way to live for Him.

On the contrary, in these verses, Paul is imploring the readers to understand that because Jesus came to set humanity *free*, we are no longer slaves answering to the demands of a slave owner, and living in fear of disobedience. Instead, we are children of God— loved and adored. Not only that, Paul says we are His heir, which culturally, for the readers at that time, was a right reserved for the eldest of a family. But Paul is letting us know that since we are adopted into God's family, we all get to have that amazing, first-born-only inheritance. In true Oprah fashion, Paul is revealing to us, "Now *you* get the full inheritance, *you* get the full inheritance, **EVERYBODY** gets the **FULL INHERITANCE**!"

Jesus changed everything. We don't just get set free from prison. We get adopted *and* get all the gifts and benefits of having a rich dad too.

It took me years to fully take hold of this freedom.

A CHILDHOOD LOST

There were a handful of circumstances—not just my tainted perspective of serving God—that led to me growing up perhaps a little too quickly, and contributed to a childhood lost.

In the years following the first encounters I had with physical violence on the streets, the storm inside of me never came to an end. Because "being mature and being strong" was so ingrained within me, I tried to be brave in the midst of teenage difficulties—reading books and listening to sermons on cassette tapes on how to deal with these situations alone in my room—and hid many of my hurts from my parents.

Throughout my whole childhood, my dad battled Hepatitis C, was rushed to the hospital every so often, and was always going through new types of treatments.

I was bullied by other students throughout junior high for being poor and overweight and, behind closed doors, was told by teachers that I wasn't smart enough for my career ambitions, or good enough for the boys I was dating. I did not tell my parents until high school.

I battled with anorexia from 7th grade until my junior year of high school, and tried to convince my parents it was only puberty. They knew I was lying and that was all confirmed once I was hospitalized, diagnosed with a blood disease, and found out that I wouldn't be able to play competitive sports again (we are a basketball family, you know the type), and that it'd be nearly impossible for me to have children.

My high school boyfriend took advantage of me sexually from my sophomore to senior year. I did not tell parents until years later.

When I was 17, the summer after I graduated high school, my dad was diagnosed with cancer. I found solace in underage drinking with my friends and hooking up with boys I did not know.

When I was 18, in the air, flying home from college to visit my dad, he passed away.

There did not seem to be a moment to have a childhood. It felt like it was one thing after the other, and anytime one painful season would end, another would begin. On top of all the things happening inside of me, there were all the things happening outside of me on the streets we ministered on and the circumstances happening amongst my family. It honestly felt like all of their hurt was a much bigger deal, and I didn't want to be dramatic and bring my little hurts up. It seemed my only choice was to grow up and to be as strong as I could be amidst my circumstances.

Wipe tears. Brave face.

PASSION POLLUTED

I took all the principles I grew up believing and lived my early adult life with this same mentality. Because of how I thought of ministry, and working within, and for a church, I never wanted to live my life that way, and never wanted to raise a family that way. I went to college seeking a different life. Years later, when God changed my life around and called me elsewhere, I said "Yes" and started writing and speaking as I do now. I knew exactly what I was signing up for.

This is not going to be fun. I know what real ministry takes.

I will be strong. No one will see me cry.

This is going to be filled with sacrifice, pain, and hardships, but one day I'll be dead and this will be over.

Be mature. Be strong. Show God you love Him.

Just like my childhood in ministry, my early adult life in ministry was founded on good principles— "God wants me to love Him, follow Him, and serve Him; it won't be easy, but God is faithful; when someone beats you up while you're preaching, get back up and lead 73 people to Jesus." You know, the usual good principles.

And yet, just like my upbringing, all these truths were tainted with legalistic extremes that made them ungodly. "If you don't do everything exactly right, someone will probably die without Jesus; if you take a day off, you better make up for it; if you take a vacation, you're just being lazy; don't show when you're weak; don't cry when you're hurt; the best way you can love God is by growing up, sacrificing everything, and having the most courage anyone has ever had."

It may sound extreme, but that's the tip of the iceberg of how I thought.

The good things I was taught were polluted by the rules I was convinced were essential to living fully for God.

STILL ONE THING

I said "Yes" to God for all the right reasons, and I said "Yes" with all my heart. For the next five years, I had an adventure of a lifetime with Him. I performed and preached on stages 3-5 days a week, and lived exclusively in hotel rooms, church apartments, and guest houses of church staff members throughout the country. God was healing my life, while taking me on a crazy expedition of knowing and falling in love with Him, His world, and His Church. Living on the road alone, and the hustle to create a career from the ground up, was one of the most difficult things I've ever done— it was lonely, scary, risky, and, at times, very painful. Still, I wouldn't trade that experience for the world. I had such special and intimate moments with God, literally in depths of canyons and on top of mountains, and met thousands of His children I would never have met otherwise. I am so grateful for that season. In those five years, God changed my whole life, inside and out.

However, there was still one thing that was not yet healed— something I didn't know that was ever wrong. I was still working like my salvation depended on it— like the weight of the world was all on my shoulders. In all those five years, I never took as many as two days out of the office (no work emails, no work calls, no online, website, or design work), and never took one week offstage. I was a slave— maybe not to the Old Testament law, like the church in Galatia, but a slave to ministry. I was in bondage to a long, made-up checklist of what it took to love and obey God, and I didn't always go about rest, relationships, and little things *like Sabbath* in the best way.

ZION

I met my husband during those five years of touring. He was a worship leader in Las Vegas at a church I was hired at for an event (he's not the one who hired me, to be clear— this wasn't a classic book-the-touring-poet-to-put-a-ring-on-it situation), and we dated long distance as I continued to travel full-time, until we tied the knot two years later. Since we dated long distance while I toured, he had no way to know what it would be like the week of our wedding and the week of our honeymoon with me taking those weeks completely off. Since I had never been married, I didn't know I was *supposed* to take those weeks off.

So I didn't. I performed at a conference in Ohio a couple days before my wedding in California. During our honeymoon, I was also working on a new line of merchandise, had phone meetings with my t-shirt designer, and was emailing and receiving bookings for my next tour. He seemed surprised at how much I was working. I thought to myself, "Doesn't he know that while we are on this vacation, people are dying without Jesus?"

I'm so glad this man stayed married to me.

For the next few months, he didn't really bring it up. I did some odd things here and there, but we were newly married and he wasn't sure how to bring it up. I, apparently, had no idea how to have relationships while having this job. One time, we crossed paths outside our house. He was on his way home from work, and I was leaving to go to the airport. He saw my suitcases and said, "Hey Sweetheart... where are you going?" I replied, "I'll be in Kansas and Missouri for two weeks—doing a mini tour there. I'll see you soon!"

When I got back from that tour, he kindly asked if I would let him know in advance when I would be gone for two weeks. I felt like that was fairly reasonable, and we never spoke about it again.

Almost a year into marriage, my husband and I started traveling together. We were in the middle of a six-month tour, driving from Idaho to Arizona, and we discovered we had an extra day between bookings. What a treat! He suggested we stop in Utah, stay the night, and finish the drive in the morning. I protested that if we drove through the night, we could get to the booking destination a day early, and we could use that extra day to do some extra work on our computers.

What fun, right?

This was the beginning of me learning of a name I was so used to answering to, I didn't even notice it.

My husband said to me, "Hosanna, you're a really hard worker. And that's amazing. That's how you've made it to where you are."

So sweet, right? But then he continued...

"I know you work really hard for God. But I don't know if you *enjoy* God."

What was this crazy man talking about?

How are people going to get saved if I just sit back and enjoy God?

He said, "Look up how far Zion National Park is. We're going to drive there, stay the night, go hiking, and just take tomorrow off to enjoy God and the world He's made for us."

The next day we hiked Angel's Landing, a 1,488-foot tall rock formation in the beautiful Zion National Park, and it was one of the most jaw-dropping and breathtaking experiences of my life. We were surrounded by various golden hues, with sunny but slightly chilly weather, and a perfect blue, slightly periwinkle sky that began collecting clouds throughout our hike. There was hardly anyone around as we walked uphill, downhill, through boulders, and amongst rocky cliffs to reach our destination. At the top, we felt invincible. We could see water streams and large trees beneath us looking like tiny toys far away.

The clouds began to drizzle us slightly.

I started to tear up.

I had dedicated my whole life to helping other people know and enjoy God and yet I myself was not indulging in His beautiful world or the incredible people around me. I almost didn't know how.

I had answered to *workaholic*, but a workaholic in church ministry, and had proudly worn that as my identity for so many years.

I knew how to hustle.

I knew how to sacrifice.

I knew how to be brave.

I did not know how to be a child.

I did not know how to have fun.

I did not know how to enjoy God.

GARDENS & PLAYGROUNDS

In Genesis 2:8-9, we see the world God originally intended for us, the home He first created for us.

"The Eternal God planted a garden in the east in Eden—a place of utter delight—and placed the man whom He had sculpted there. In this garden, He made the ground pregnant with life—bursting forth with nourishing food and luxuriant beauty. He created trees, and in the center of this garden of delights stood the tree of life and the

tree of the knowledge of good and evil." (VOICE)

God first created a playground.

He didn't create a church building. He didn't create an office. He created a beautiful, restful, fun-filled, open-aired garden, blooming with color and life.

In Judah Smith's book, *How's Your Soul?*, he states:

"In our fixation with keeping rules and appeasing a God we secretly suspect might be angry or disappointed, we are in danger of losing one of the fundamental keys to a healthy soul: that of rest, of enjoying who God is and what he has created for us. God wants to remind us how imperative rest and enjoyment are for our souls, so the first description we get of the garden is that the foliage is fun to look at and the food tastes amazing."[9]

Why was I spending so much of my life over-working, when God originally created the world for us to enjoy it, each other, and Him?

Why was I so obsessed with being a hard-worker for God, and forgetting to rest and take delight in spending time *with Him*?

Why had I spent so many years being a slave to ministry, a slave to productivity, a slave to my check list, and never taken the time to soak in this verse in Galatians and allow it to seep into my life?

"You are no longer a slave but God's own child."

I had been answering to the wrong name.

In the MSG translation, Galatians 4:4-5 is put this way:

"...God sent his Son, born among us of a woman, born under the conditions of the law so that he might redeem those of us who have been kidnapped by the law. Thus we have been set free to experience our rightful heritage..."

There's that word again— *kidnapped*.

For many of us, our childhoods have been kidnapped.

Our ideas of God, our ideas of the world, and our ideas of ourselves have been kidnapped.

For the church in Galatia, their idea of salvation was kidnapped.

And in many ways, ours has been too.

God is not looking for slaves.

He is looking for children.

Salvation does not come through legalism, religious rituals, or never taking a vacation.

Salvation comes through faith in Jesus— faith like a child.

What does it mean to be a child?

To lounge around in grassy fields and just enjoy the sunshine?

Yes.

"God, my shepherd!
I don't need a thing.
You have bedded me down in lush meadows,
you find me quiet pools to drink from.
True to your word,
you let me catch my breath
and send me in the right direction." (Psalm 23:1-3 MSG)

To be free of the weights of responsibility?

Yes.

"Come to Me, all who are weary and burdened, and I will give you rest." (Matthew 11:28 VOICE)

To be reckless? To be risky? To be curious? And yet somehow be safe?

Yes.

"The minute I said, 'I'm slipping, I'm falling,'
your love, God, took hold and held me fast.
When I was upset and beside myself,
you calmed me down and cheered me up." (Psalm 94:18-19 MSG)

To play with your friends all the time?

Yes.

"How good and pleasant it is when God's people live together in unity!" (Psalm 133:1 NIV)

To just be joyful and have fun everyday?

Yes.

"Always be full of joy in the Lord. I say it again—rejoice!" (Philippians 4:4 NLT)

To not be constantly anxious about the future and always worrying about the burdens of the world?

Yes.

"Give your entire attention to what God is doing right now, and don't get worked up about what may or may not happen tomorrow. God will help you deal with whatever hard things come up when the time comes." (Matthew 6:34 MSG)

To care only about enjoying and laughing and resting and leaving all the cares of the world to the adults?

Yes.

"Live carefree before God; he is most careful with you." (1 Peter 5:7 MSG)

God is saying to each of us, "Come, be a child. Celebrate all the time. Trust that I am watching you, will carry you, and always want good things for you. Find safety in me. Don't wear the burden of being in charge. Enjoy the world I created for you. Enjoy life with me. Enjoy life with my other children."

I wish I had known during my elementary, junior high, and high school years that is was okay to be sad, it was okay to be weak, and it was okay to seek help and ask for comfort. I wish I had known when I was 18 that I didn't have to be strong right after I lost my father. I wish I had known that I did not have to hide my hurts or be ashamed of the things done to me. I wish I had known during my first five years of ministry as an adult that I could work hard, hustle, and be obedient to God, and still have rest, relationships, and fun. I wish I had known that not only was all of that *okay*, but God *wanted* to comfort me, *wanted* to be my strength, *wanted* me to take vacations *(c'mon somebody!)*, and wanted me come to Him like His sweet, expectant, and joyful kid.

I had grown up quickly in vain. I was always supposed to approach God as a child.

A CHILDHOOD FOUND

Years later, this verse, Galatians 4:7, has revolutionized my life.

I am no longer a slave to my checklists. I am no longer a slave to my fears. I am no longer a slave to my old names— "Workaholic," "Ministry Addict," "Never Weak," "Always Stressed," "Grew Up Too Fast," or "Proving Myself."

It took me some time to get here, but finally— I am beginning my childhood.

I am beginning a life of recklessly trusting God, and unapologetically enjoying the people and the world around me. I am *making space* in my work schedule, my travel schedule, and my social calendar to be young, have fun, run in waves, binge on Oreos, ask out people to lunch just because I want to, fly to another state to watch a TV show season premiere with my friends, go on lots of dates with my husband, try new things that scare me, indulge in God's Word—not just for work and not even to find something in particular but just to know more about Him— watch that movie I keep meaning to see, plan a trip with my friends, visit my brother, take career risks that sound insane but could be really fun, work with people who make me laugh, make me happy, and make me better, write run-on sentences that are long and improper because they are fun and because I can, take a run around the block because it's sunny and beautiful and because I feel like it, and just live in a state of not taking myself too seriously. Instead, I am becoming aware of all of the beauty, sweetness, and life-giving joy that God places around me, and diving into it, because *He loves that,* and He delights in our delight.

In Psalm 103:5, King David writes:

"He fills my life with good things.

My youth is renewed like the eagle's!" (NLT)

God wants to fill all of our lives with good, wonderful, and enjoyable things. No matter where we find ourselves—no matter our current ages, our current locations, or our current circumstances—God is calling each one of us *His child*.

Will we answer to a life of enjoyment?

Will we answer to a life of trusting Him?

Will we answer to a life of not carrying the weight of the world on our shoulders?

Will we answer to a life free from anxiety and worry?

Will we answer to a life of relying on God and not on ourselves?

Will we answer to a life of being in awe of God, expectant of wonderful things—the good things He has for us—and believing anything is possible?

Will we answer to a life where we are loved— not because of what we do, but because of who we are?

For many of us, it's time to begin our childhood.

For many of us, it's time to answer to— "Child of God."

QUESTIONS

What were some ideas from your childhood (whether through your own assumptions or things you were taught) that you now see were incorrect?

What were some ways your childhood was taken from you or situations that made you grow up too fast?

Have you ever felt a slave to a checklist for God? If so, what has your checklist been and how have you tried to hit those marks?

What are some differences between a slave and a child?

What were times in your life when you were not enjoying God?

What were you doing instead?

How would your life look different if you lived it through the lens of enjoying God and enjoying His people?

For you, what habits, perspectives, or decisions would you need to change in order to live more like a child— delighting in, trusting in, and resting in God?

ACTION

What is something fun you would like to do this week in order to enjoy God, enjoy His people, or enjoy the world around you?

Think of a park you could visit, someone to take to breakfast, a date you could surprise your spouse with, a shopping date you could have with your daughter, a night out you could plan with your friends, a coffee shop you have been wanting to try out or read a book in, a trip to the beach, or a hike in the mountains. Be creative. Or be simple.

What is something that would fill up your soul and give you childlike joy?

Think of that thing. Commit to doing it this week. Call that person, make that plan, and *enjoy*.

Our victory begins when we stop answering to "slave" and start answering to "God's child."

Our victory begins when we claim back—and for some of us, begin—our childhoods.

OUR VICTORY BEGINS AS WE BEGIN TO DELIGHT IN, TRUST IN, REST IN, AND *ENJOY* GOD.

"
THE NAMES THAT
MY FATHER
ETERNITY'S AUTHOR
THE WORLD'S
CREATOR
HAS CALLED ME
ARE THE ONLY
NAMES THAT I
ANSWER TO…

"

CHAPTER 07
UNCHAINED

Our victory begins with surrender.

That's not always the war strategy we tend to expect.

But it's the key to winning the war over our lives.

We've exposed the Enemy. We've listed our old names, taken control of our soundboards, chosen to come back from defeat, got back into the race, and made the decision to fight. We've read the names God has said of us and have learned what He really thinks of us.

Now it's time for our victory.

Surrender is the first step.

SURRENDER

There is no lasting, life-changing victory over our old names without the power of Jesus living inside of us.

We can explore all the names God gives us and memorize all the scriptures we want, but it all means nothing if we are unwilling to let go of our old names, our old identities, and our old mentalities, and lay them at the feet of Jesus.

We cannot begin to walk in liberty unless we lay down the things holding us back.

We cannot live as free men and women with chains still holding us down.

So what are the things we are still holding onto?

This I know to be true— whatever we are chained to, Jesus Christ has come to set us completely free. Not a little bit free. Not mostly free. Not free on Sundays. Not free from *some* chains. 100% free.

Our victory begins here— when we make the decision to surrender our chains, our sins, and our hurts to a Victorious Savior.

So what are we chained to?

Are we chained to who we used to be— plagued by memories and things we did a long time ago, living in prisons of shame because of who we *were*?

Are we chained to what people once did to us—haunted by things that were said about us, done to us—things people did that would break God's heart, but somehow, they put the blame back on us? Are we are living in prisons of abuse, embarrassment, and defeat?

Are we chained to people's expectations— living most of our days feeling like we always miss the mark and we'll never be good enough no matter how hard we try? Are we living enslaved to standards we feel are out of reach?

Are we chained to religion— holding tight to a list of Do's and Don'ts, hoping we can get by with just the bare minimum? Are we marking our legalistic checkboxes, worshipping rituals instead of worshipping God, and living in prisons of traditionalism without a real revelation of who Jesus is?

Or.

Are we chained to our own sin— feeling like we know what we want to do, what is right to do, but somehow we feel out of control and we still do the opposite? Are we living in a prison of our own flesh, feeling like there is no way to be free?

What are *you* chained to?

What is holding you back?

Identifying these chains will enable us to throw them down and move forward in victory.

I don't know about you, but I know each of these chains very well.

At one point or another, I've been in bondage to each one.

I've been a slave to what I've done, a slave to what was done to me, a slave to what people expected of me, a slave to traditionalism, and a slave to my own sinful desires. I lived like these chains were a part of me, as if they were a part of my skin, always attached to me, and like I had no other choice but to live this way. These prisons became like a home— the walls were bars, but I had a roof and a bed and I was comfortable there.

Maybe you feel this way.

Maybe you feel as if these chains will always be a part of you.

Maybe you've already decided that while there are some chains you'd like to be free of, others would be impossible to let go of fully.

I resonate with those feelings.

For most of my life, I lived with these chains because I never fully understood who Jesus was and what He did for me.

I didn't understand that He didn't come to restrict me.

I didn't understand that He didn't come as a police officer throwing a set of rules and regulations at me.

I didn't understand that He didn't come to condemn me, but rather, because of sin, I was already condemned.

So Jesus came... to be a friend. He came to give His life and set all of His friends free.

Turns out, Jesus is nothing like who I thought He was.

Turns out, I don't have to live the way I thought I had to either.

More than anything, it turns out I was living in a prison of false presuppositions— false assumptions of who Jesus was and of who I could be.

The truth is that because our friend came, died, was buried, and was raised to life— this changes *everything*.

When we choose to surrender to Jesus, and invite Him to be the King of our fight, the King of our identity, and the King of our hearts, there is a victory waiting for us.

"...Christ lives within you, so even though your body will die because of sin, your spirit is alive because you have been made right with God. The Spirit of God, who raised Jesus from the dead, lives in you. And just as God raised Christ Jesus from the dead, he will give life to your mortal bodies by this same Spirit living within you." (Romans 8:10-11 NLT)

The *same* Spirit that raised Jesus? The *same* God who resurrected the Savior of the world from the dead? Not a different version? Not a less powerful version? Not a watered-down version? No. The same power—the same miracle—the same God who raised *Jesus* will give us life too.

He will set us free from our chains *too*.

He will set us free from the pains of our past *too*.

He will set us free from who we were and give us a new life *too*.

Because Jesus had the victory over the grave, we too can live victoriously.

Who knew that our lives could be far better than what we've settle for?

Whenever we feel like maybe our sins are too great or our pasts are too sad or our chains are too strong, we must remember this:

If God is not enough to raise us from the dead, if He's not enough to save us from our lives of sin, if He's not enough to redeem us from all the places we've been, the things we used to do, and the person we used to be—

Then He *couldn't* have been enough to resurrect Christ.

Either we have been made alive. Or Jesus is still dead.

If we are still choosing to live in chains, then each day we are living our lives as statements that Jesus has not risen from the grave.

"...If there is no resurrection of the dead, then Christ has not been raised. And if Christ has not been raised, then your faith is useless

and you are still guilty of your sins. In that case, all who have died believing in Christ are lost! And if our hope in Christ is only for this life, we are more to be pitied than anyone in the world. But in fact, Christ has been raised from the dead. He is the first of a great harvest of all who have died." (1 Corinthians 15:16-20 NLT)

Since the tomb that Jesus was buried in is *empty* and no Savior's bones are lying amongst some graveyard, we can know and rest assured that death has long been conquered.

Since He is alive, we are alive. Since He has the victory, we have the victory.

Our chains can fall to floor.

Yes, we were once slaves, but we are bound no more.

Yes, we were once dead in our sins, but we are buried no more.

We can choose to come alive. We can choose to be free. The same Spirit that raised Jesus can resurrect each one of us— today.

Turns out, these chains are *not* a part of us. They never were.

They were merely accessories.

And they are out of style.

It's time to toss them. They never looked good on us anyway. Let's update our wardrobes. It's a brand new season. It's a brand new day.

"Then, when our dying bodies have been transformed into bodies that will never die, this Scripture will be fulfilled: 'Death is swallowed up in victory. O death, where is your victory? O death, where is your sting? For sin is the sting that results in death, and the law gives sin its power. But thank God! He gives us victory over sin and death through our Lord Jesus Christ." (1 Corinthians 15:54-57 NLT)

O death— *how you like me now?*

O sin— *where* is *your power?*

O chains— *now who is boss?*

God gives us victory over sin and death through Jesus.

The Enemy's victory *already* ended when Jesus died for our sins, our old ways, and our old names.

Our victory *already* began when Jesus rose from the dead and gave us the opportunity to rise from our graves— to lay down our old ways, and to instead, choose a new name and a new life with Him.

If we want to claim this victory, we can choose to do so today.

The battle begins on our knees.

We don't have to have it all figured out in this moment.

Our victory simply begins with the choice of surrender.

QUESTIONS

What have you been chained to?

For some of us it's one big thing. One giant chain. We hear this question and we know, I am chained to _____.

For others of us, it's many things. We are aware every day of multiple shackles wearing us down, holding us captive, overwhelming our thoughts, and disabling us from living the life that we want to.

What are ways that you might be chained to whom you used to be?

What are ways that you might be chained to something that was done to you?

What are ways that you might be chained to what people expect of you?

What are ways that you might be chained to religion without a true revelation?

What are ways that you might be chained to your own sin?

How would your life look different if you lived every day like Jesus was actually alive and resurrected from the grave?

ACTION

Now that we know what the Bible says of us, what God thinks of us, and the new life that is available to us, it's our choice to respond.

My encouragement to you is to make that choice.

Surrender the hurts in your life.
Surrender the sins in your life.
Surrender the fears in your life.

Stop holding onto to these chains like they are your skin.

It's time to let go of whatever is holding us back.

In your own words, talk to God, and tell Him what you are feeling chained to. Tell Him what you want to surrender to Him. Ask Him to take those chains, set you free, and make you new. If you believe Jesus died and rose from the dead, tell God you believe that, and tell Him you want to live a resurrected life too.

This is between you and God. Surrendering to Him is the most important step to victory. Setting you free from your pasts, your hurts, and your chains is one of His favorite things to do. He'd love to. I hope you make that choice today.

OUR VICTORY BEGINS WITH SURRENDER.

―

BECAUSE JESUS HAD VICTORY OVER THE GRAVE, WE TOO CAN LIVE VICTORIOUSLY.

CHAPTER 08
CHANGING NAMES

God is in the business of changing names.

He loves getting rid of the old and starting something new.

He loves taking our endings and giving us beginnings.

He loves canceling our old identities and giving us brand new ones.

But God cannot redeem a fake version of ourselves.

And God cannot make us new if we don't ask Him to.

God changes names when we come to Him as we *really* are.

God changes names when we identify, receive, and declare who *He* really is.

HERE'S TWO

There are a handful of stories in the Bible where God changes someone's name.

That's a powerful thing. When God changes a name, He's changing His description of that person. When God changes a name, it's altering more than just what that person is called; it's altering their identity. And because identity influences who we become, when God changes a name, He's changing someone's future.

Here are two stories—one from the Old Testament, and one from the New Testament—where God changed someone's name. They teach us two different steps to God changing ours as well.

PREVAILED

In the Old Testament, we meet a man named Jacob.

Jacob was a twin, and when he and his brother Esau were born, Jacob came out of the womb grabbing onto his brother's heel. So his mother gave him a name which means "he takes by the heel."[10a] For the rest of his life, we see Jacob doing just this— trying to pull his brother back or pull himself ahead. Because Esau was born first, he was entitled to an exclusive birthright and blessing reserved for the eldest. One day, when they were adults, Jacob made a good bowl of soup and his brother Esau was so hungry that when Jacob told him he'd give Esau a portion in exchange for his birthright, Esau took the deal. That's quite a payment. This was no bowl of Campbell's soup (no hate); Jacob must have been on another level of culinary greatness.

Later in life, Jacob goes after Esau's blessing. The twins' father, Isaac, was growing old, and the Bible says **"his eyes were so that he could not see"** (Genesis 27:1 NIV). He tells Esau to make him some food and when he comes back he is going to give him his blessing. Esau leaves and while he is gone, Jacob—that heel grabber—comes in to steal this from his brother too. He dresses like his brother, puts animal fur around his skin (because Esau was a hairy beast of a man), and when his father asks, **"Who are you?"** Jacob replies: **"I'm Esau, your firstborn son."**

Jacob was a little manipulator. He conned his brother with soup for his birthright, and now he is straight up lying to his own father to get a blessing that is not his. His father asks again, **"Are you really my son Esau?"** Jacob answered, **"I am."** (Genesis 27:18, 19, 24 VOICE)

He was portraying himself as someone he wasn't.

He was masking himself with another identity.

Then his father blessed him, but he didn't bless the *real* him. He blessed what Jacob was pretending to be.

Is that really a blessing if it's all pretend?

Esau was furious, and rightfully so. I can't even imagine if I did this to my older sister. I'm getting chills just thinking about it. He is so enraged that he wants to kill Jacob, so Jacob *runs*. First good idea we've seen Jacob have so far! Actually, I can't speak to how wise that was but that's definitely what I would have done. Jacob runs from the scene to another land, and for the next handful of years, has a totally different life. He gets married—twice—he has goats, sheep, almonds, kids, he has a whole new thing going on, but he's still running. He got the blessing, but he has not yet confronted his lie and is still living in fear for when his brother finds him.

Is it really a blessing if you're still on the run?

Years later, Jacob reaches out to Esau, and Esau comes to meet him. While Jacob waits for him, terrified and nervous for his life, he pleads with God, **"Deliver me from the hand of my brother!"** (Genesis 32:11a DRA)

The night before Jacob sees Esau for the first time in years, Jacob has an encounter with God. He sends his family to go ahead on the journey, and the Bible tells us this:

"...But Jacob stayed behind, left alone in his distress and doubt. In the twilight of his anguish, an unknown man wrestled with him until daybreak."

We don't know if the man *was* God, an angel, or another type of messenger of God, but we know he was *from* God.

"When the man saw he was not winning the battle with Jacob, he struck him on the hip socket, and Jacob's hip was thrown out of joint as he continued to wrestle with him.

Man: Let me go; the dawn is breaking.

Jacob: I will not let you go unless you bless me.

Man: What's your name?

Jacob: Jacob."

Here we see Jacob ask for a blessing, and then identify himself as he really is.

Not his brother's name.

Not the name he wishes he went by.

His real name.

"Man: You will no longer go by the name Jacob. From now on, your name will be Israel because you have wrestled with God and humanity, and you have prevailed."

Jacob: Please, tell me your name.

Man: Why do you ask what my name is?

Right then and right there the man blessed Jacob." (Genesis 32:24-39 VOICE)

The messenger from God asked Jacob who he was, and when Jacob answered truthfully, *the messenger blessed him.* For so long Jacob had been lying. For so long Jacob had been running. But there he was on the eve of confronting his greatest lie, his greatest regret, and we see him come clean with his reality. Then the messenger of God said, **"Now your name will be Israel,"** which means "one powerful with God,"[11] "one who strives with God," or "you have striven with God and with humans, and have prevailed."[10b]

The next morning, Jacob and Esau reunited, Jacob approached his brother humbly, and the two reconciled.

Jacob becomes a father to many nations— his 12 sons become the 12 tribes of Israel.

We want a new name? We must be honest about who we really are.

I love how Pastor Steven Furtick, lead pastor of Elevation Church in Charlotte, NC, puts it: "God can't bless who you pretend to be."[12]

We learn from Jacob that in order for God to change our name—the identity we answer to, the identity we live by, the identity we are known as—we must first approach Him humbly and honestly.

Jacob identified who he was. Imperfect. A liar. A heel-grabber.

Who are you really?

God wants to bless and renew the real you.

ROCK

In the New Testament, we meet Simon— another man who had his name changed. This time it was Jesus who provided a new name after Simon identified who *Jesus* was.

Simon was a fisherman, a working man, and co-entrepreneur with his friends, James and John, and a disciple and friend of Jesus. He was a charismatic, strong-willed risk-taker. But flawed as any human man. Many of us could relate to him. One of the stories he's known best for is when he attempts to walk on water.

In Matthew 14, we read of Simon on a boat with his friends when a storm comes in, and from the shore, Jesus begins walking on water. Jesus invites Simon to join him, and Simon does— very bold and risky indeed. But as soon as he sees the crazy waves beneath him and gets fixated on the storm surrounding him, Simon is overcome with doubt. Then he sinks, and Jesus saves him. Many of us can resonate to these very human—sometimes bold but sometimes fearful—emotions of Simon.

We read about his name being changed in Matthew 16:13-18:

"When Jesus arrived in the villages of Caesarea Philippi, he asked his disciples, 'What are people saying about who the Son of Man is?'

They replied, 'Some think he is John the Baptizer, some say Elijah, some Jeremiah or one of the other prophets.'

He pressed them, 'And how about you? Who do you say I am?'

[Simon] said, 'You're the Christ, the Messiah, the Son of the living God.'

Jesus came back, 'God bless you, Simon, son of Jonah! You didn't get that answer out of books or from teachers. My Father in heaven, God himself, let you in on this secret of who I really am. And now I'm going to tell you who you are, really are. You are Peter, a rock. This is the rock on which I will put together my church, a church so expansive with energy that not even the gates of hell will be able to keep it out.'" (MSG)

Jesus asked Simon to identify *Him*.

Forget whatever everyone else was saying— Who did *Simon* say Jesus was?

Simon replied that Jesus was the Christ, the One who came to rescue humanity, the Messiah, the Redeemer the prophets had promised, the Son of the living God, the One who came to pay for the sins of the world. Simon declared who Jesus was! And then Jesus gave him a new identity as Peter— a rock and foundation for His Church.

Jesus can't save us, redeem us, and complete us, unless we identify, receive, and declare that He is the Savior, the Redeemer, and the Completer who can.

Forget what everyone else is saying— Who do *we* say Jesus is?

This is one of the most important questions any of us will ever answer.

Undoubtedly, what we think about Jesus reflects what we think about ourselves.

If we don't think He's the Forgiver of our sins (Ephesians 4:32), perhaps that's why we don't think of ourselves as Forgiven.

If we don't think He's the Healer of our brokenness (1 Peter 2:24), perhaps that's why we don't think of ourselves as Healed.

If we don't think He's the Savior of the world and the Hope for all humanity (1 John 4:14), perhaps that's why we don't think we can be saved and why we feel hopeless.

Either I am everything Jesus has said, or Jesus is not who He says He is.

Our victory not only begins with the choice to surrender our chains to Jesus, but it continues with the choice to declare who Jesus is to us, and to find our identity in *His* name.

Whenever I am struggling with doubt, stress, or seemingly impossible situations in my life, I ask myself, "Who do I say Jesus is?"

Identifying who He is reminds me of who I am. Reminding myself what I know of His power, love, and authority reminds me of the peace and the victory that I have.

Because He is the Rescuer, I am Rescued.

Because He is the Savior, I am Saved.

Because He is Love, I am Loved.

DECIDE AND DECLARE

Jacob identifies himself.

Simon identifies Jesus.

The man who once manipulated his family and the man who once sank in waves of doubt— both are given new identities. Both are given a new purpose.

Have we come to Jesus as we are?

"If we claim we have no sin, we are only fooling ourselves and not living in the truth. But if we confess our sins to him, he is faithful and just to forgive us our sins and to cleanse us from all wickedness. If we claim we have not sinned, we are calling God a liar and showing that his word has no place in our hearts." (1 John 1:8-10 NLT)

Have we made the decision of who Jesus is to us?

"If you openly declare that Jesus is Lord and believe in your heart that God raised him from the dead, you will be saved. For it is by believing in your heart that you are made right with God, and it is by openly declaring your faith that you are saved." (Romans 10:9-10 NLT)

Some of us might believe that Jesus is the risen Savior, but we are not living like He is. Some of us might believe that the name of Jesus has power, but we are not daily declaring His name over our circumstances as if it does. Some of us might need to remind ourselves who Jesus is in order to repeatedly and confidently identify ourselves fully with Him.

THERE IS POWER IN THE NAME OF JESUS.

I love the words to this song, "What a Beautiful Name" by Hillsong Worship:

You have no rival, You have no equal
Now and forever, Our God reigns
Yours is the Kingdom, Yours is the glory
Yours is the Name, above all names
What a powerful Name it is
What a powerful Name it is
The Name of Jesus Christ my King
What a powerful Name it is
Nothing can stand against
What a powerful Name it is
The Name of Jesus[13]

Something I love about the name of Jesus?

It's greater than my name.

Something I love about the identity of Jesus?

It's greater than my identity.

Something I love about who Jesus is?

He is always the same.

"Jesus doesn't change—yesterday, today, tomorrow, he's always totally himself." (Hebrews 13:8 MSG)

Even though I am constantly changing. His character is the same. His point of view is the same. And when I identify myself with Him— I am identifying myself with someone steady, certain, and sure. In Him I have found the greatest certainty, the greatest confidence, and the greatest peace I have ever known.

As we come as we are, He changes us.

As we come to Him as He is, He changes us.

Even in our uncertainty, our fragility, and our weakness—

There is power in the name of an unchanging, unwavering Jesus.

Alright one more worship song— my husband is a worship pastor and I am constantly experiencing God in new ways through singing these words to Him, so get excited, this isn't the last song I'll reference in this book.

Elevation Worship has a song called "Call Upon the Lord." Here are the words to the beautiful bridge:

Jesus' name will break every stronghold
Freedom is ours as we call His name
Jesus' name above every other
All hail the power of Jesus name14

I love that.

His Name is greater than any name.

My name.

Your name.

Their name.

Our old names.

Any names ever.

Jesus name above all the others.

All hail the power of a life-changing, chain-breaking, freedom-giving, unparalleled, unmatchable, beautiful name.

QUESTIONS

In the current state of your life, do you identify more with Jacob or with Simon? In what ways do you relate?

Why do you think it's sometimes hard to come to God as we really are?

Why do you think it's sometimes hard to identify who He is to us?

Have there been moments in your life where you thought God was one thing, but later in your life, you thought He was something else? What are the different things you have thought about the character of God and the person of Jesus?

How does what you think of Jesus change how you think of yourself and your circumstances?

ACTION

It's one thing to surrender our chains to Jesus. It's another to declare that is He is who He said He was, and to proclaim with our own voice that He is the Lord of our lives.

In your heart, think on who you really are, and come to Jesus just as that.

In your heart, decide on who you think Jesus—the Son of God—really is, what He is capable of, the power He has, and the role you want Him to have in your life.

Tell Him.

For many of us, we need to tell Him each morning and declare who He is before we get out of bed.

I encourage you to practice proclaiming the position He has over your circumstances, and begin your days in a posture of recognizing His power, and worshipping His name.

My challenge to you is to consistently— honestly, vulnerably, and confidently, come to God as you are, and tell Him who He is to you.

OUR VICTORY BEGINS WHEN WE MAKE THE CHOICE TO DECLARE WHO JESUS IS TO US, AND TO FIND OUR IDENTITY IN HIS NAME.

> THE ENEMY HAS NO POWER HERE PERFECT LOVE CASTS OUT FEAR AND PERFECT LOVE HAS NAMED ME AND YOU.

CHAPTER 09
LEARNING "J"

When I married my husband, I changed my last name to his.

Days before our wedding, we went to a nearby city hall to get our marriage license. We each filled out forms stating who we were, our legal information, and the names of the family we came from. We paid a fee, signed a document—probably had some long meaningful moments staring blissfully into each other's eyes—and I filled out an additional form stating the new name—his name—I was to now take on and identify with.

Later that week, I wore a beautiful white dress (that was $90 at a vintage boutique by the way, hey-o!), I walked down an aisle (it was actually a staircase—a metaphorical aisle—it counts), I stood in front of our friends and family, and I said "I do."

I said "I do" to a life with a man whom a few years before I knew nothing about.

I said "I do" to a life with a man who had changed my perspective on the world and made me the absolute best version of myself.

I said "I do" to a life with a man who was giving, strong, kind, patient, courageous, humble, confident, hilarious, hard-working, risk-taking, and selfless— and cared about Jesus more than his ego and people more than his paycheck.

He was everything I wanted to be like. I was so proud to be his wife—proud in a totally bragging, "Can you believe the cool guy I got to marry me?" not-humble-at-all kind of way. I was proud of the family he came from and to now be bearing his name.

I said, "Yes." And I said it with all my heart.

And yet.

It took me a long time to get used to that new name.

For my entire life up until that point, I had answered to one name. I had signed my signature with one name. I had perfected the perfect cursive "W" at the beginning of my maiden name to be gracefully drawn like trendy typography upon my checks, documents, and receipts.

And now, I had to learn how to draw the perfect "J," the first letter of my new last name.

It wasn't exactly a graceful process.

When I heard people talking of me and calling me by my new name, I was not always sure I felt like I identified with it. It didn't sound like me. It sounded like they were speaking of a totally different person.

Some of my best friends wouldn't (and still haven't, you know you are) change my name in their phone, jokingly (maybe some not jokingly) in protest. Hearing enough of my peers still call me by my old name made me reminisce on that old identity, the good ol' single years we spent together, and what it represented to me and to them.

When I heard my old name called, I would still answer to it.

When I heard my new name called, I would often forget that was me.

I was accidentally writing my old name on checks and forms and would have to scribble them out.

No matter how much I practiced it, my "J" was still really messy.

I started to feel like I would never get used to this new name.

SLOPPY J'S

When we make the decision to answer to a new name in Christ, we often go through this same thing.

We said, "Yes." And we said it with all of our hearts.

But sometimes it takes a while to get used to our new identity.

Sometimes it can feel unnatural to be our new selves.

For most of our lives, up until this point, we have answered to an entirely different name— a name we, naturally, were used to. It has been our identity. People know us by our old name. Not all these old names are necessarily bad. For some of us, our old names were *good*. They were just not the *great* that we have now found in Jesus.

Perhaps some of us are not proud of how long it has taken us to get used to this new name.

When we hear our old name called, sometimes we still answer to it.

When we hear our new name called, sometimes we forget that is us.

When we hear people talking about us and calling us by our new name, we are not always sure we can fully identify with it. It doesn't sound like us. It sounds like they are talking about someone totally different.

Some of our friends won't let go of "those good ol' days." Some still hold tight to who we were before this decision and what it represented to them.

Every now and then, we accidentally identify with our old name.

And no matter how much we are trying to practice it, our signature—our vernacular, our mentality, the way we represent ourselves—is still really sloppy, and not up to the standard we dreamed it would be.

We can start to think, "Has my victory really begun?"

We can start to think, "Is this new identity real?"

We can begin to feel like we'll never get used to this new name.

WHEN HAVE I EVER?

I thought for sure my husband was growing impatient with me. I assumed that he was thinking I was protesting my new last name, that he was embarrassed that I was not the perfect wife, and was hoarding in all of his anger because I was not instantly used to this new name I signed up for.

But he wasn't.

When I brought it up to him, he said to me, "Hosanna, I could not care less."

I know— he's so dreamy and romantic. It's a wonder he's not also a poet.

He continued, "When have I ever done or said *anything* that would make you think I'd care about what your responses or signature would look like to other people?"

He was right.

Looking back, it was pretty weird that I thought he was going to be so angry. All of my fears were assuming he wasn't all of the things I said "I do" to. Didn't I remember the man I married? I was consumed with all of this unwarranted fear, which his character—who he consistently was and had always been—completely contradicted.

Finally, he turned to me, and in the most practical, obvious, and understated way he said, "You've had a totally different name your whole life, of course it would take you a reasonable amount of time to get used to this name."

That had never occurred to me. I had spent over 20 years used to a totally different name— *of course* I was not going to be used to this new name overnight! What he cared about was not how my "J" looked when other people saw it— maybe it wasn't perfect, and maybe it did show how new to marriage I was. He only cared that I was still walking in my vows, and that I was still proud to be his.

You see, he was there—

When I walked towards him in a white dress, amongst our friends and family.

He was there—

When I said "I do" to a life with him.

And he *is* there—

As we make the decision every day to work at a healthy, fun, and God-honoring marriage.

He was there, he remembers these moments, and he knows the reality of my character and how hard I work towards this commitment.

He could not care less what other people were calling me or the moments when I accidentally signed my old name. He cared about the commitment we made to each other. He cared that every day I received his love, and every day I was doing my best to give that love back.

WHEN HAS HE EVER?

We often think God must be growing impatient with us, tired of how long we are taking to be an outstanding Christian, annoyed by how often we think of our old lifestyle, and hurt by every time we forget our new name or accidentally answer to our old one.

Our idea of God acting that way or thinking of us that way is also pretty weird. The greatest source we have about who He is and what His character is like towards His children is the Bible, and everything it says completely contradicts our fears. Here's what it has to say about God's character:

"God is sheer mercy and grace;
not easily angered, he's rich in love.
He doesn't endlessly nag and scold,
nor hold grudges forever.
He doesn't treat us as our sins deserve,
nor pay us back in full for our wrongs.
As high as heaven is over the earth,
so strong is his love to those who fear him.
And as far as sunrise is from sunset,
he has separated us from our sins.
As parents feel for their children,
God feels for those who fear him.
He knows us inside and out,
keeps in mind that we're made of mud.
Men and women don't live very long;
like wildflowers they spring up and blossom,
But a storm snuffs them out just as quickly,
leaving nothing to show they were here.
God's love, though, is ever and always,
eternally present to all who fear him,
Making everything right for them and their children
as they follow his Covenant ways

and remember to do whatever he said."
(Psalm 103:8-18 MSG)

In the VOICE translation, Psalm 103:8 states:

"The Eternal is compassionate and merciful.
 When we cross all the lines, He is patient with us.
 When we struggle against Him, He lovingly stays with us…"

Then there's Ephesians 2:4-5, which says:

"…Because of his great love for us, God, who is rich in mercy, made us alive with Christ even when we were dead in transgressions—it is by grace you have been saved." (NIV)

And Hebrews 4:14-16 tells us:

"Since we have a great High Priest, Jesus, the Son of God who has passed through the heavens from death into new life with God, let us hold tightly to our faith. For Jesus is not some high priest who has no sympathy for our weaknesses and flaws. He has already been tested in every way that we are tested; but He emerged victorious, without failing God. So let us step boldly to the throne of grace, where we can find mercy and grace to help when we need it most." (VOICE)

Here's the gist. God is not impatient with us at all.

He is not the angry, white-bearded man with wings of glitter we once imagined he was, lounging in a pool of clouds yelling at us from the sky with a digital echo effect on his resounding voice. He is not looking forward to making us pay up for every second we fell short. He is super loving, extremely gracious, and hates holding grudges. In fact, just as we read in Chapter 5, He loved us *so much*, that *while* **"we were dead in transgressions,"** He sent His Son Jesus to die *for us*, to make us alive through Christ, and to give us a second chance at being in a relationship with God for forever. God **did not even wait** for us to make the decision to choose Him before He demonstrated His love towards us!

And as it turns out, Jesus is also not the drill sergeant we imagined Him to be, unsympathetic to the process of turning away from our old lives and shocked when we still have flaws. He totally gets it. We are worrying in vain. There is no reason for us to assume that we need to have it all together—to be perfectly and consistently used to our new name—in order to be loved and adored by God. We should approach God boldly, knowing that mercy and grace is waiting for us, all the time, no matter what.

When we said "I do" to this commitment, to this new name, that's the kind of God we said "yes" to. That is what His character is actually like.

We said "I do" to grace and mercy.

We said "I do" to patience and kindness.

We said "I do" to a never-quitting, never-changing, always-forgiving, everlasting kind of love.

Why have we been living in fear assuming that He is anything different than who we thought He was when we first chose Him? Don't we remember who our God is?

HERE COMES THE BRIDE

"Husbands, you must love your wives so deeply, purely, and sacrificially that we can understand it only when we compare it to the love the Anointed One has for His bride, the church." (Ephesians 5:25 VOICE)

The Bible compares our relationship with Jesus to that of a bride and a groom. We, those who love Him, have chosen Him, and are a part of His Church, are the Son of God's bride— *the love of His life*. Even more than my husband and his patience and understanding with me, Jesus loves us so much that He is not obsessing over the fact that this new name of ours is taking a while to get used to.

All he cares about is that we made the decision. All he cares about is that we made the vow. All he cares about was that we said "yes," we said it with all our hearts, and every day we are working towards owning that identity, and enjoying this new life together with Him. He is not concerned with how new or old this relationship is or how it's perceived to others. He cares that we are still walking in our vows, that we are still proud to be His, and that we have not changed our minds about our decision.

He is not changing *His mind* based on what other people are calling us.

He cares about the commitment we made to each other. He cares that every day we receive His love, and every day we are doing our best to love Him back.

He was there, and He remembers that day, how we approached him (whether by real aisle, staircase aisle, or other metaphorical aisle, no judgment), and that decision we wholeheartedly made to answer to a new name and to identify with a new family.

NEVER GIVING UP

In Philippians 3:9-14 (VOICE), the Apostle Paul states what His heart desires more than anything and where he is in that process.

What he desires:

"When it counts, I want to be found belonging to Him, not clinging to my own righteousness based on law, but actively relying on the faithfulness of the Anointed One. This is true righteousness, supplied by God, acquired by faith. I want to know Him inside and out. I want to experience the power of His resurrection and join in His suffering, shaped by His death, so that I may arrive safely at the resurrection from the dead."

Where he is on that journey:

"I'm not there yet, nor have I become perfect; but I am charging on to gain anything and everything the Anointed One, Jesus, has in store for me—and nothing will stand in my way because He has grabbed me and won't let me go. Brothers and sisters, as I said, I know I have not arrived; but there's one thing I am doing: I'm leaving my old life behind, putting everything on the line for this mission. I am sprinting toward the only goal that counts: to cross the line, to win the prize, and to hear God's call to resurrection life found exclusively in Jesus the Anointed."

Just like Paul, our greatest desire should be for our identity to be found in belonging to Jesus. For our obsession to not be with good works or righteous deeds, but for the safety in our Salvation to be reliant on our faith in Jesus, our trust in who He is, and our decision to follow Him. To know everything about our Groom, our Savior, God's Son, Jesus Christ, and have a whole new life because of Him.

And just like Paul, this is where we are on this journey— we have not fully achieved all of this yet. We are not yet flawlessly answering to our new name. Our lives are still under construction. But we have not given up. We are still charging on, determined to grasp everything Jesus has for us. Maybe we are not doing everything exactly how we should be doing it every single second. But we *are* leaving our old lives and old names behind and making a vow to commit our lives to this Savior and to this purpose. Let us keep sprinting to the only thing that counts, not how quickly we can identify with our new name, not how quickly we can perfect our cursive "J," but instead, the ultimate prize, the ultimate goal: a completely new name and an entirely new life in Jesus that we get to enjoy on this side of Eternity, and the next.

It's okay that we're not there yet. The point is that we have not given up.

Be patient with yourself. Give yourself grace. God is patient with us, and His love and His grace have no limits.

NEW CONFIDENCE

It's been some years since I said "I do" to my husband, and certainly, over time, I have grown more accustomed to my new name. I have met many people since then who have only known me as this new name, and when they hear my old name, they think *that* sounds weird. I have successfully gone years without ever referring to myself as my maiden name (major win there), and I now fully identify with this new name. Completely safe in the love my husband and I have for each other, and the hard work we intentionally put into our marriage, I am confident in this identity.

This process of becoming a new creation may take some time. But eventually, people meet us and greet us only as the name we answer to now, and can't *believe* the things we used to do or the person we used to be when we answered to that old name. There have been times when I've shared stories with my husband about some of the events in my past, and some of my old ways, and many of them he can't imagine— they're so different from the woman he met me as. I don't blame him. Even to me, it can sometimes feel like I'm talking about an entirely different person.

We eventually start answering to our new name more than our old name. We begin to realize how safe we are in God's arms of love and grace, and as we continue to work diligently and intentionally on knowing Him and identifying with Him, we grow confident in this identity.

Soon, our new name will become our only name.

"Let us then approach God's throne of grace with confidence, so that we may receive mercy and find grace to help us in our time of need." (Hebrews 4:16 NIV)

Our victory is here when we are not living in guilt, insecurity, and fear, but rather living in the freedom we find in God's love.

Our victory is here when we do not give up on our pursuit to grasp ahold of all the good things God has for us.

Our victory is here when we are living our days safe in this certainty: we belong to Him.

Let us be patient with ourselves.

Let us not give up.

Let us not be discouraged.

Let us approach God—and all His mercy and grace—with confidence.

QUESTIONS

What is an example of an identity in your life that took a while to get used to?

What helped you get used to that name?

When you think of the kind of person you want to be, what are certain character traits that have seemed out of reach?

When you think of names that God gives you, what are specific names that have felt like would they would be impossible or more difficult than others to fully embody?

Why do you think some identities take longer than others to get used to?

ACTION

Have patience with yourself.

You already made the decision for a new name and a new life.

Keep making that decision to the best of your abilities.

Keep working towards that decision to the best of your abilities.

Keep answering to the names that God calls you, that you want to be, even when you don't feel fully there yet.

God has so much grace on us.

More than we can ever imagine.

Have grace on yourself today.

**WHEN WE DO, OUR VICTORY BEGINS...
AND GOD'S VICTORY IS HERE.**

PART III —

GOD'S VICTORY IS HERE

CHAPTER 10
THE DANCE

I did not get to dance with my dad at my wedding.

In many ways, sin stole my dance from me.

My dad was a gangbanger, thief, pimp, molester, and heroin addict, infected with Hepatitis C from a dirty needle, and, as I mentioned earlier in this book, died of three forms of cancer when I was 18.

Though he died sober, clean, in love with Jesus, and having been an incredible minister to the outcasts of San Francisco, the repercussions of the sin in his own life and the ripple effect of his choices eventually took their toll. I deeply mourned the loss of my father, the absence of my best friend, the reality of a fatherless life, and the future thought of a wedding without a father-daughter dance— a dance he and I had frequently talked about.

But this is not a sad story.

One of my dad's prayers during the last days of his life was that I would never be fatherless.

It seemed his prayers were left unanswered that one afternoon in March when I ran into his room to find him lifeless and cold. It seemed as if my hope—my dance—had been lost forever.

I began to answer to the name, "Fatherless."

I tried to find solace in alcohol, promiscuity, status, and image.

I was underage, but I partied. A lot. Alcohol became my god. There were times I had a bottle of alcohol hidden under my pillow (in my Christian college dorm room), just to take a sip from every now and then so I could forget who I was and what I had lost. I was already touring within the underground slam poetry scene, speaking angrily about all my pains and brokenness. As I traveled from booking to booking, I hooked up with men and women in back alleys, bars, and clubs all around the US, finding a sense of thrill in the loss of my identity, exchanging intimacy with people whose names I didn't know. I spent my time with people just as angry as me and just as passionate at finding ways to *forget*.

People told me it was normal— that I was a victim of a fatherless generation and that, statistically speaking, all my behavior was to be expected.

Turns out, many other people were answering to "Fatherless" too.

Eventually though, I grew tired of the girl in my mirror that was half-living.

I started to seek the Father—the ultimate Father—desperate for a life far better than this. He was still there, and He was still available. Slowly but surely, as I sought after Him, I found a Hope, a Love, and a Security I had never known. I called out to Him. I'll be honest, "calling out" sounds a little prettier than it was. It may have been a few days of anger/crying/screaming. I told Him I hated how painful every day was, I hated how I was living, I hated who I turned out to be. And that I was sorry. I told God I was desperate for something better, and I knew He had it.

Indeed He did. He came to my rescue. He brought with Him all of the forgiveness, all of the patience, and all of the understanding anyone could fathom. The comfort I felt was like coming up for air. I latched onto Him with every piece of me. I quit the lifestyle I had worshipped for so long. No matter how much work it was going to be (and yes, it ended up being a massive amount of work), I was choosing to change my life around.

I told you— this is not a sad story.

OPEN DOORS

For the next few years of my life, I began touring as a spoken word artist *now* talking about the joyful, wonderful, crazy love of God. During these years, dozens of men, pastors, and mentors came alongside of me in absolutely the most pivotal seasons… and became like fathers to me.

I met them on different sides of the country, in different situations, and for different reasons. Many great men, along with their wives and children, accepted me into their families as their own, believed in me, advocated for me, challenged me, and gave me a second chance at a childhood— a second chance to be seen through a father's eyes.

Here is something crazy: none of these men were raised with perfect examples of Godly fathers in their own lives. They each have their own stories of what they missed in their childhoods.

So how did they become such great men?

How did they become such great *fathers*?

At one point in their lives, they too sought the ultimate Father.

At one point, they made a decision to be different than the examples they'd been given.

At one point, they chose to answer to a new name.

And because of their decisions, they became *such* great men, that when a fatherless, wandering, homeless poet came across them, she felt the love of her Heavenly Father undoubtedly bursting straight through them, and chose *them* to fill the gaps the Enemy had made, *them* to reclaim what the Enemy had stolen. Because God was so strongly alive inside of them, they became like His hands, His feet, His mouthpiece, and His reflection— protecting, loving, and encouraging this fatherless girl. It was these fathers and their wives who opened up my heart to love again and challenged me to let people in. It was these families who encouraged me to continue obeying the call of God to travel the country telling this story, no matter how unconventional my journey was. It was these mirrors of the love of God who never let me quit and always opened up their homes for me in moments when I wanted to.

It was the stories of these men choosing a new identity that opened up the doors for me to be who I am today.

We too can make the choice they made. We too can be what no one ever was to us. We can change patterns around. We can seek *the* Father, love people the way He does, and be the examples the world needs to see of redeeming, forgiving, and unending love.

Statistics have no power in this story.

GIRL, PUT YOUR RECORDS ON

Years later, I married my incredible husband—the one who waited for me to learn "J," the one who brought me on top of Angel's Landing.

As we planned our wedding day, he told me that the tradition of the dances was my decision— whatever I wanted to do, was alright with him. My amazingly kind mother-in-law also told me it was okay if we left out both of the dances all together— the father-daughter dance and the mother-son dance. Our families were both incredibly gracious towards me and allowed me to have the wedding day I wanted.

I had a choice.

What name was I going to answer to?

At our wedding, four fathers danced with me— all men who at different points in my adult life played major roles in my beliefs in God, in love, and in a new identity. When I had no one, I had these fathers and their wives. When I hated God, I had their family's love for me and their love for God carrying me through. When I didn't believe in love, marriage, and intimacy, their marriages and families reminded me of what was possible.

We danced to the joyful, soulful, free-spirited tune of Corinne Bailey Rae's "Put Your Records On," and at different parts of the song, each man cut in.

As each father spun me around the dance floor, it was like God's own hands and feet were sweeping me away. As the music played, it was if God's own voice was singing, "You are not alone. You are surrounded." As the attendees watched, they were not seeing an absence of a role on that special day but instead, there was a surplus of fathers on this dancefloor.

I had never seen redemption clearer.

I had never understood John 10:10's **"life abundant; *superadded*"** in a more obvious way.

My dad's prayers were answered. I was not fatherless. I had sought the

Father. And though I had wandered for quite some time, I eventually found my way back to the dancefloor.

GOD'S VICTORY

For many of us, sin has stolen our dance.

Our mother left us. Our boyfriend cheated on us. Our purity was stolen from us. Our dad was an alcoholic. Our best friend was a liar. We've been told we're not good enough. We've been told we're not pretty enough. We've been told we're not strong enough.

We've been told we're a victim of our circumstances.

Satan has been lying to us, stealing from us, and trying to destroy us from the ground up. He likes that we think we are a fatherless generation. He likes that we think there is no hope in the world. He likes that we think that we are products of the sin in our lives, the victims of the sins of our families, and the consequences of the sin in our world.

And yet, the Word of God says the opposite.

King David writes, **"Father to the fatherless, defender of widows— this is God, whose dwelling is holy. God places the lonely in families; he sets the prisoners free and gives them joy."** (Psalm 68:5-6a NLT)

God's victory is here. In filling the gaps of our lives. In creating families. In giving us a renewed joy.

If we let Him in, God will redeem what Satan has snatched from us. He will be the Father we don't have. He will be the Best Friend we lost. He will provide for us a home, a family, a freedom, and an ultimate, eternal, exuberant joy. He will out-do what the world has done. He will bring healing to our brokenness. He will give us unwavering victory.

So no, this is not a sad story. But what kind of story is it then? How does it end?

It ends with the choices we make.

What name are we going to answer to?

Are we going to be better than the examples that came before us?

Are we going to wholeheartedly seek the ultimate Father, strive to look like Him, love others like Him, and choose to be the fathers, mothers, sisters, brothers, teachers, and mentors to others that we never had?

Are we going to choose to reclaim what sin has stolen?

Are we going to start a new ripple effect of love, kindness, and compassion for the generations that follow us?

We are not statistics. We are not victims. We are not powerless over our identities.

Who will we choose to be?

COACH

After I danced with those four amazing dads, I danced with my awesome brother-in-law (Go Warriors), and then ended my dance with my little brother, Elijah.

I love my little brother. He's 10 inches taller than me and calls me his little sister, but whatever. This is my book— he's my little brother.

Elijah was 12 when we lost our father.

He was the first one to grab on to me and hold me as I was falling to my knees, finding out about our daddy, and screaming in tears at his bedside.

He was also the last one spinning me on the dancefloor at my wedding that beautiful autumn day.

Elijah is now a leader in our family's ministry, has a high position in retail, and is a basketball coach to inner-city boys.

The love of God is strongly alive in him. I am so proud of the man he is, and I am continuously learning from him.

One day, I asked him why he's so passionate about coaching. Where did this drive come from?

He answered me, "None of those boys will grow up and say they didn't have a man in their life cheering them on. I will be there. Coach Elijah will be there."

We can choose to turn this cycle around.

Elijah to me is the definition of a statistic demolished.

He chose to not to answer to "Victim"— what people expected of him, what statistics predicted of him. He chose to answer to a completely different identity and to walk in it with confidence.

He chose to not answer to "Fatherless." He chose to answer to "Coach."

As he chose a new name, he was choosing an entirely new purpose in life.

Just like the fathers who danced with me.

Just like I aim to choose every day of my life.

I refuse to be called "a fatherless generation."

I have power over my story. I have power over my choices.

My Father is here.

My Father is available.

My Father restores broken lives.

Through my Father, I reclaim the dance that sin had stolen.

My Father— His song plays on. We can choose to dance again.

God's victory is here— in the open doors, on the basketball courts, and on this dancefloor.

QUESTIONS

Who are people you know that made a choice to answer to a new name, changing the trajectory of their life?

How have you seen their decision influence the lives of others?

Who has opened doors for you?

Who has been a "coach" to you?

Who have you chosen to come alongside of you on the dancefloor of life?

ACTION

What is a choice you can make to redeem what the Enemy has stolen from you?

Honestly take a minute to reflect on a decision you can make to open doors for others, be a "coach" to someone in need, or to reclaim a sad story for God's glory.

GOD'S VICTORY IS HERE WHEN WE ARE LIVING UNDEFINED BY WHAT HAS HAPPENED TO US, WHAT WE LACKED, OR WHO WE WERE, AND INSTEAD, ACTIVELY LIVING IN A NEW PURPOSE.

> WHEN YOU STOP ANSWERING TO YOUR OLD NAMES THEY STOP HAVING POWER OVER YOU.

CHAPTER 11
FIGLESS

God's victory is here when we take off our masks.

God's victory is here when walls that divide us fall, when veils that hide us tear, and when truths that we have kept in the dark come out into the light.

God's victory is here when His people are living lives of honesty and authenticity, free to be simply and sincerely... ourselves.

And yet.

If we're being honest?

Many of us live in fear of showing who we *really* are.

Many of us would rather curate a false image that comes off as impressive and untouchable.

Many of us would rather be architects of walls, rather than wrecking balls that break down division, as long as the barriers keep our true selves hidden.

Let's be honest.

Many of us are spending more time on our mask... than our actual identity.

PROJECT RUN(A)WAY

We are not the first ones.

Here's where it started.

When Adam and Eve believed Satan's lie, disobeyed God, and ate the fruit, they felt so much shame that their instinct was to cover themselves up. Prior to this moment, they were naked, exposed, and free, just as God made them, but now we find them hand-making clothing out of fig leaves. Here we see the first fashion garments in history. How wild is that? Whenever I see fig trees I get emotional. I've been known to tell strangers at my local plant shop, "Do you know what this leaf represents?" It's a great conversation starter. Most of the time. Sometimes I get too into it and it can get weird. I won't defend that part. But I'm obsessed with this story.

Adam and Eve's first reaction to their shame was to cover up and hide.

And we are no different.

Because of the things that we've done in our past, our shortcomings, and the insecurities we have about ourselves, we too have become accustomed to the craft of covering up.

We fashion together these fig leaves—these masks, these lies, these false identities—hoping that they make us worthy enough to approach God, approach people, and approach our mirrors. We run from people that call out and expose truths within us. We do our very best to keep the realities of our lives hidden— how we really feel, what we really did, what really scares us, and what we are really like.

Many of us are playing dress-up, wearing fig leaves to this world-wide masquerade ball, praying no one sees the real us beneath all the façades.

We are wasting our lives away trying to impress each other, instead of knowing each other; trying to out-do each other, instead of coming together; and trying to cover up our truths and see who can fashion the most attractive lie, instead of embracing the beauty of what is real.

Instead of living as children of God, wonderfully made and intentionally purposed, we're acting as craftsmen, spending more time and energy on our costumes than our character, more time and energy on our masks than our mindsets, and more time and energy on the image we want to portray than in the person we really are.

If people love the fake version of us, is that really love?

If the false image we're portraying is successful, is that really success?

I'd argue that it's far easier to be impressive than it is to be authentic. It's far easier to be successful than it is to be vulnerable. It's far easier to get other people's likes than it is to like the person that you see in the mirror. The shallow status that we are aiming for is far too easy to obtain.

Don't you want to achieve a confidence that is real and will last? Isn't your identity worth the effort?

We read earlier that Jacob struggled with this same thing— masking his true self, working on his garments, crafting together animal hair to place around his body, pretending to be his brother in order to get a blessing that wasn't his. Only when he came to God as he really was, did he receive a rightful blessing *and* a new name— one that was his for the rest of his life. Only when Jacob came humbly and honestly before God and before his brother Esau, was there true reconciliation in their family's relationship.

The smallest doses of true intimacy and authentic community are far superior to the even the largest portions and highest levels of elitism and impressiveness based on manufactured identities.

God's victory is here— even in that small dose.

In his challenging book, *Scary Close*, Donald Miller writes,

"I don't mean to overstate what is yet unknown, but part of me believes when the story of earth is told, all that will be remembered is the truth we exchanged. The vulnerable moments. The terrifying risk of love and the care we took to cultivate it. And all the rest, the distracting noises of insecurity and the flattery and the flashbulbs will flicker out like a turned-off television."[15]

Why are we wasting our time decorating masks and perfecting made up names that will not last?

For many of us, the names we are answering to aren't necessarily bad— they just aren't real.

Aren't we tired of designing, curating, and walking down the world's runway wearing a version of ourselves that we know deep inside isn't us at all? Aren't we done wasting time that could be used towards being a person we are proud of?

A BETTER COVERING

God did not create us to live in hiding.

I like to say He created us *figless*— free from masks, free from lies, free from shame; exposed, honest, and authentic. (If any of this sounds familiar— it is; I'm plagiarizing myself. I wrote spoken word album—and then wrote a devotional—called *Figless*. I told you I loved this story. If you dig spoken word, check it out. You can discuss it with all the people at my local plant shop; they're tired of hearing me talk about it.)

God created us to be free from anything that would separate us from Him and divide us from each other. That means free from guilt, free from insecurity, and free from feeling like we need to be anything other than whom He created. God always intended for us to live free. And even after we humans fell short, that was *still* God's desire. He still wanted to enjoy life with all of us closely, personally, and as the true people He made us to be.

So, He sent down a different kind of covering. Something that would last longer than our fig leaves. We thought we needed to be covered? We were right.

"...Without the shedding of blood, sin cannot be forgiven." (Hebrews 9:22 VOICE)

Enter: Jesus.

Our fig leaves were not sufficient. What man couldn't do, Jesus did it.

"Yes, Adam's one sin brings condemnation for everyone, but Christ's one act of righteousness brings a right relationship with God and new life for everyone." (Romans 5:18 NLT)

The shame of our sins we once covered in leaves, Jesus has fully covered with His blood.

With this kind of powerful, groundbreaking, game-changing, life-giving blood covering us completely, the only natural response is to live our lives in a constant mindset of fearless, unashamed liberty. Until we realize the power of Jesus' blood, we have no idea how free we are.

This doesn't mean that we ought to put every aspect of our intimate lives on display. This means that the fake display we have become intimate with is obsolete and purposeless when Jesus' blood has covered us in a real, freeing, and lasting way.

Shame has been erased. Guilt has been crushed. Fear has been obliterated.

His blood is stronger than the fig leaves we use to cover the things of our lives that we're not proud of. This covering is better than the fake personas we use to mask what we're ashamed of.

God's victory is here when we stop hiding ourselves behind lies, stop placing impressiveness over truthfulness, and start living as the free men and women He made us to be.

"Don't lie to one another. You're done with that old life. It's like a filthy set of ill-fitting clothes you've stripped off and put in the fire. Now you're dressed in a new wardrobe. Every item of your new way of life is custom-made by the Creator, with his label on it. All the old fashions are now obsolete. Words like Jewish and non-Jewish, religious and irreligious, insider and outsider, uncivilized and uncouth, slave and free, mean nothing. From now on everyone is defined by Christ, everyone is included in Christ." (Colossians 3:9-11 MSG)

We are done with that old life.

We are done being fake.

We are done living divided.

We are done parading around with false names— we're over wasting time on keeping up with our fake selves.

These fig leaves belong in the trash with our chains— they are outdated, out of season, and no longer fit us well.

Let's stop hiding our truths.

Let's cross the bridge that Jesus' blood has built— the bridge to God and the bridge to each other.

Let's throw down our masks.

Let's throw down our lies.

Let's throw down our shame.

God created us to live lives of authenticity and freedom.

Let's live free again.

The runway is over.

The masquerade has been canceled.

It's time to wear something far more beautiful.

Every one of us is to be defined by Christ, clothed in Christ, and covered in Christ.

QUESTIONS

What tactics do people use to cover up the truth about themselves, their lives, and their insecurities?

What is scary about taking off our masks? What are we afraid of?

What are areas in your life that you feel you already walk in freedom, free from a false façade?

What is an area in your life where you could be more honest, vulnerable, or authentic?

Practically, what would it look like to start fully living a "figless" life, without masks, without shame, without lies?

How would the world be different if we didn't walk around with masks or false identities?

ACTION

We were never meant to live alone, and we were never meant to do life covered up in fear.

Think of a way you could take down a mask this week.

Perhaps think on a fear, a worry, or a story you may be hiding, or embarrassed to bring into light. Perhaps think of one person you could share this with. We don't have to put every aspect of our intimate lives on display, our business is not everyone's business, but we will become freer when we start to share our hidden truths with those we trust. They can also keep us accountable and speak good things into our lives.

The goal is to identify an aspect of your life in which you want to be more real, and then to actively work towards authenticity in that aspect.

Think on what that would look like for you.

Think on joining a small group.

Think on saying sorry for something you've hidden.

Think on changing a habit that has created a façade.

Think on sharing something you've held inside of you.

How can you live more "figless" this week?

GOD'S VICTORY IS HERE WHEN WE TAKE OFF OUR MASKS, SPEND MORE TIME ON WHO WE ARE THAN WHO WE ARE PERCEIVED TO BE, AND LIVE AS GOD INTENDED US TO LIVE— HONEST, AUTHENTIC, AND FREE.

**SHAME
HAS BEEN
ERASED.
GUILT
HAS BEEN
CRUSHED.
FEAR
HAS BEEN
OBLITERATED.**

CHAPTER 12
VINTAGE BOOTS

I used to mask my deepest hurts and my greatest insecurities.

Then these seven words changed my life.

"I have this pair of Vintage Boots..."

SECRETS

At one point in my life, it was my biggest secret.

Some of the old names I used to answer to were "Unworthy," "Ugly," and "Undesirable."

As I mentioned in an earlier chapter, I was badly bullied as a kid and secretly battled eating disorders for most of junior high and high school. I thought if I looked a certain way, people would approve of me and those old names would be erased. After growing sickly thin and regularly fainting from the lack of nutrients, I was hospitalized. Through my rehabilitation, doctors told me that it would be nearly impossible for me to have children. Though I had battled anorexia and bulimia as a way to get rid of my old names, it seemed as if I had only made matters worse. I now felt even more unworthy, but this time, it came with a great deal of shame. I grew used to wearing these names as my identity—after all, I was only a child when I first heard them; I practically grew up with them.

I felt a lot of guilt for caring so much about what other kids thought of me, a lot of shame for what I had put my body through, and a lot of insecurity about the outcome. At 19, I got re-checked by another doctor and was given the same diagnosis. The doctor assured me, "Most women who put their body through what you put yours through are never able to have children. Don't worry; it's not rare."

What did she want me to think? "Wow... I'm so glad I'm not rare"?

Good grief. I was a *child*. Where are people's social skills?

Though many women— including some of my closest friends—have lived the reality of infertility and child loss, it isn't widely socially acceptable to talk about, even in this day and age. Thus, our shame stays covered up and our truths are whispered in hushed tones. This is not something that makes most people very comfortable. This is not something that makes most women feel gorgeous, flawless, or supremely desirable. For many of us, it's our biggest secret.

How could we share about a name we've been told for so long is ugly?

THE BOOTS

When I was 19, I briefly opened up about this truth of mine for the first time while speaking at a girl's conference in Anaheim, CA. Though I only hit on it for a second, and quickly moved on, I was so overcome with emotion from saying it out loud at all, that when I got into my car after the event, I turned on my recorder. It was a common thing I did at the time, freestyling into a recorder as I drove or walked or whenever I could. I bawled my eyes out as I spilled out the truth that I was holding inside. I freestyled (or recklessly poured out emotions like floods being set free from the walls of the Hoover Dam) the piece that is now known as "Vintage Boots."

This piece, the most raw and honest thing I had written (or spoken) at the time, was about a pair of boots I had been saving for my daughter since high school.

BEHIND THE BOOTS

I was a vintage clothing fanatic as a teenager, and my mom would always make fun of my fashion choices, commonly saying, "I used to own something like that when I was a kid! It was ugly then and it's ugly now!" We bonded through thrift shopping together throughout my junior high and high school years, loving a good bargain hunt, and always making fun of each other's varying clothing choices. I still love running around thrift stores with my mama. In 2005, I bought a pair of vintage boots that quickly became my favorite shoes. I wore them everywhere.

My mom would tease, "I used to have those kinds of boots back in the 70s!"

I would joke back, "Then why didn't you save them for me?" Over the years I began to joke that I was saving these "ugly" boots for *my* daughter. And over time, I stopped wearing them completely, preserving them and taking care of the old leather in the hopes that, one day, a little girl would wear them.

In my piece, I speak about saving these boots... even after I was told I was saving them in vain.

This piece was the first time I really admitted the truth about what was going on inside of me. The doubts. The embarrassment. The confusion I felt knowing this so young, when most women in my position were much older. The uncertainty of my future.

I ended up memorizing this freestyle/emotional waterfall and performing it at a small venue in Anaheim later that week. The owner of a lounge in Beverly Hills (whose wife had battled infertility for years) was there and asked me to perform it at his venue the next week. I was eventually asked by multiple venues, clubs, and open mics to perform at various events all over the area. I performed at underground poetry slams, headlined at concerts, was featured in shows all over the Los Angeles and Orange County area, and quickly became known as "The Girls with the Boots." Many times, people didn't even know my real name. It wasn't too long until I was performing "Vintage Boots" all over the state, then at the Bowery Poetry Club in New York, then all over the US, then at the Great Wall of China in Beijing, and later put it on my first album in 2013, *Maps, Boots, and Other Ways We Get There*.

Up until this point, I had actively performed poetry for years. I grew up doing it. Why was *this* the piece that an audience all of a sudden connected with?

It was honest. And real. And people crave honesty.

We are so over the perfect, flawless, fake images of people we see not only in the media but also in our own lives.

We are desperate for authenticity.

The one thing that made me feel the most disgusting, the most vulnerable, and the most uncomfortable was actually the one thing that connected the most with people. That wasn't my dream, and that wasn't my plan. But this is why I kept performing that piece: there has never been one time in all of these years of performing "Vintage Boots" where there wasn't at least one woman who was going through exactly this and needed to know she wasn't alone.

It turns out, we like hearing we're not alone.

It turns out, we *do* need to know that we aren't rare.

It turns out... there is a purpose in my *old name* after all.

RECYCLE

God's victory is here when we turn our old names into vehicles to help set others free.

Even when we have made the choice to answer to a new name, that doesn't mean our old name doesn't have a purpose.

Perhaps, our old names are not trash. Maybe instead, they can be recycled.

God wants to use our victory to help others find their victory.

COOK

We live in a world of secrets.

Instead of sharing with each other and knowing each other, we are whispering around each other. Are we trying to impress people? Do we want them to think we are not broken? Better than them? Above them looking down? We are so busy trying to be who we think the world wants to see, when who we really are, where we've really been, and what we're really struggling with is what will actually bridge the gap and create true community.

It is within our power to be the solution. We can be better than a world of secrets. We can be a world without strangers. Within the honest sharing of our stories, we can cure the world's disease of loneliness.

This poem, "Vintage Boots," began what is now my lifelong goal of exposing lies, sharing secrets, and proclaiming truths.

Those seven little words changed my life.

I see the world differently. I see old names differently.

I see hurts not as broken pieces, but as an open links to connect to someone else.

I see stories that Jesus redeemed as opportunities to answer to "God's Messenger to the World."

Years later, many of my deepest hurts, fears, and ugly pictures of my past are on display. "Vintage Boots" is now far from the most revealing or the most uncomfortable of stories I speak of in front of an audience. And certainly, some stories are still more difficult to share than others. I'm okay with that. Vulnerability is a journey. But I know now more than ever that the truth sets people free. I know when I share my truths, no matter how hard it may be, I get to be a part of freedom.

That's worth stretching for.

That's worth risking for.

That's worth living for.

Freedom is far more important than our fears.

What about you?

Have you spoken out loud about your past, your brokenness?

Are you using it to set others free?

Are you being a beacon of realness and honesty in your own community?

Truly, this is *something rare*. But with every person who tells the truth, others are inspired to tell their truths, and then others do the same until the ripple effect of honesty has freed us all from the walls we have hidden behind.

Authenticity is one of the most contagious things in the world.

People don't want to be alone. People don't want to be impressed. People want to be free.

What's your biggest secret?

What's your deep hurt?

What's your great insecurity?

It could start with you.

People are starving for honesty, realness, and authenticity.

Feed them.

Keep cooking.

Within your story is the power to set someone free.

QUESTIONS

What is an item or a place that holds a significant meaning or memory to you? What does it represent?

Do you think the story of the item or place could relate to someone else?

Do you have stories from your childhood or past that have been difficult to share?

Why do you think honesty is contagious?

Why do you think people's honest, personal stories impact others in such big ways?

Can you name a person who shared something vulnerable that impacted you in a significant way? Perhaps a speech you heard, a book you read, or something someone shared with you one-on-one? What about what they said impacted you?

ACTION

What is an old name of yours that you could share to help someone else?

How could you go about doing that?

Perhaps it's reaching out to someone that you know is going through the same thing.

Perhaps it's writing a song about it and sharing it at an event.

Perhaps it's writing a blog about it and sharing it online.

Perhaps it's sharing it at a bible study or at a church event.

Perhaps it's opening up about it with your co-workers, sports team, or peers.

Think honestly about how you can use your old name and the story of God's victory in your life in order to help someone else have victory in theirs.

Take a minute to ask God for new ideas on how and where you could share your story.

GOD'S VICTORY IS HERE WHEN WE USE OUR OLD NAMES TO HELP PEOPLE FIND THEIR NEW NAMES.

—

**WITHIN
YOUR STORY
IS THE POWER
TO SET
SOMEONE FREE.**

CHAPTER 13

HEAVEN ON EARTH

We need not wait any longer for God's victory to begin.

God's victory is here. And God's victory is now.

A NEW POSTURE

I once thought, I had missed out on all the fun and frivolous things of childhood. I once thought—as that college student told me that day my dad was beaten—that life on Earth was a place of pain and hardship, and we just had to wait until Heaven to be happy. I once thought, I had to wait out, push through, and endure all these old names, all these old hurts, and all these old identities until I died, and then— finally! I would get all the new things.

Then a verse drastically changed my life.

In this passage of Scripture, Jesus is teaching His disciples how to pray.

It's a very simple prayer. Amongst the few requests to God that He gives them, Jesus prays:

"Your kingdom come, your will be done, on earth as it is in heaven." (Matthew 6:10 NIV)

It must be intentional— the specific words Jesus, the Son of God, includes when teaching His people how to address our Father God.

It must be deliberate— anything He mentions in this model prayer.

It must be important— to pray that God's kingdom comes and His will is done on Earth as it in Heaven.

Here we find that it is possible for aspects of what we wait for in Heaven to be brought down to manifest *during our lifetime* on this planet.

Here we find that perhaps we don't have to wait until death to experience the joys that God has for us in a heavenly realm.

Here we find the posture in which we can approach God and approach our time here on Earth.

And yet.

Is this how we're praying?

Is this how we're living?

ON EARTH AS IT IS IN HEAVEN

If Heaven is a place where we are in a continuous state of worshipping God (Revelation 5:13) and enjoying His presence (Revelation 21:3), why—on this Earth—are we making so little time for either? Why do we prioritize so many other things?

"On Earth as it is in Heaven."

If Heaven is a place where we see God personally, know God intimately (1 Corinthians 13:12), and are continuously resting in Him (Revelation 14:13), then why are we spending more time working for Him than seeking, talking to, and finding rest in Him?

"On Earth as it is in Heaven."

If Heaven is a place of inclusion, unity, and unending community, why are we spending so much time on Earth being divisive? Revelation 7:9-10 tells us that the crowd in Heaven was **"too huge to count. Everyone was there—all nations and tribes, all races and languages,"** worshipping God together. (MSG)

"On Earth as it is in Heaven."

If Heaven is a place of banquets, feasting, and tables filled with people from all nations, with one Father, one God, in common, eating well together (Matthew 8:11), then why aren't we looking for more ways to embrace community? Why aren't we creating more opportunities for the children of God to circle up and eat, share, and enjoy together? Why aren't we planning more dinner parties?

"On Earth as it is in Heaven."

If God's will being done is an intricate definer of what Heaven is like (Matthew 6:10), then why here on Earth are we so obsessed with the wills of others? Why are our goals and desires more human-focused than Heaven-focused? Why are our decisions based on our own wills, agendas, and preferences over His?

"On Earth as it is in Heaven."

Are we living our days in line with this prayer?

Or have we simply lost sight of Heaven?

C.S. Lewis says that it is "since Christians have largely ceased to think of the other world that they have become so ineffective in this. Aim at Heaven and you will get earth 'thrown in': aim at earth and you will get neither."[16]

For far too long, many of us have focused our eyes on how to succeed on earth, utilizing our time figuring out how to accomplish earthly status quos, and spending many of our days in worry, doubt, competition, insecurity, sadness, fear, depression, and as victims to circumstances in our past.

But that's not Heaven.

That's Earth.

"So if you're serious about living this new resurrection life with Christ, act like it. Pursue the things over which Christ presides. Don't shuffle along, eyes to the ground, absorbed with the things right in front of you. Look up, and be alert to what is going on around Christ—that's where the action is. See things from his perspective. Your old life is dead. Your new life, which is your real life—even though invisible to spectators—is with Christ in God. He is your life. When Christ (your real life, remember) shows up again on this earth, you'll show up, too—the real you, the glorious you..." (Colossians 3:1-4 MSG)

It's time to stop staring at the ground and to cease fixating our eyes, our emotions, and our goals on the things of this earth.

It's time to look up.

It's time to stop seeing things from the view of our old life— that life is dead, gone, cancelled, and demolished.

Our new life with Jesus is our real life.

It's time to be more of who we already are.

A NEW NAME

There's something else we know of Heaven.

Revelation 2:17 says, **"... to the one who conquers through faithfulness even unto death, I will feed you with hidden manna and give you a white stone. Upon this stone, a new name is engraved. No one knows this name except for its recipient."** (VOICE)

If we get a new name in Heaven, then why are living our lives on Earth still defined by any old ones? If we're the only one who will know our new name, then why are we allowing any other human to name us here on Earth?

Scholars have a lot to say on the significance of our name being put upon a white stone.

Some believe the white stone is referring to the ancient Greek custom of "giving a white stone to those acquitted on trial and a black stone to those condemned." The white stone then represents a token of innocence, a symbol of a clean slate, and a stamp of purity.[17]

Some believe the white stone represents victory. White stones were awarded to "the conquerors in the Olympic games, with their names upon them, and the value of the prize they won."[18]

Some believe the white stone is connected to the Ten Commandments, which were moral laws written by God (Exodus 32:16). This would be a symbol of God proclaiming our character as He proclaimed His with the engraving of stones.[19]

Each of these symbols are possibilities because they each echo truths the Bible has already said of us and of God.

We know we have been gifted the removal of guilt because **"the blood of Jesus, [God's] Son, cleanses us from all sin."** (1 John 1:7 NLT)

We know that **"overwhelming victory is ours through Christ, who loved us."** (Romans 8:37 NLT)

We know that God says of those who **"choose to do what pleases [Him] and commit their lives [to Him]: 'I will give them—within the walls of my house—a memorial and a name far greater than sons and daughters could give. For the name I give them is an everlasting one. It will never disappear!'"** (Isaiah 56:4b-5 NLT)

We can be certain— the white stone with a new identity is given **"to everyone who is victorious."** (Revelation 2:17 NLT)

To all who have the victory, a new name is given.

"On Earth as it is in Heaven" looks like living with an identity that God has given you... that no one can take from you. We are pure, we are victorious, and God has declared our new character.

EVERYTHING IS NEW

Answering to a new name means living with a new perspective—God's perspective—and bringing the perspective of Heaven down to Earth.

I think a lot about Heaven.

I think about Heaven when I think about my dad.

I think about Heaven when I think of my future.

I think about Heaven when I'm overwhelmed by the burdens of this world.

Revelation 21:3-7 is one of my favorite passages about Heaven. It reminds me of my reality. It's the perspective I try to hold onto.

"I heard a voice thunder from the Throne: 'Look! Look! God has moved into the neighborhood, making his home with men and

women! They're his people, he's their God. He'll wipe every tear from their eyes. Death is gone for good—tears gone, crying gone, pain gone—all the first order of things gone.' The Enthroned continued, 'Look! I'm making everything new. Write it all down—each word dependable and accurate.'" (MSG)

It continues...

"It is done! I am the Alpha and the Omega, the beginning and the end. I will see to it that the thirsty drink freely from the fountain of the water of life. To the victors will go this inheritance: I will be their God, and they will be My children." (VOICE)

If I am praying for God's kingdom to come and for God's will to be done on Earth as it is in Heaven, then I am living with this confidence everyday of my life—

In Him, everything is new.

In Him, I am new.

In Him, I am victorious.

In Him, I have an inheritance.

In Him, I am the child of the Creator of the universe.

Death is defeated.

Tears are wiped away.

Pain has lost.

God's presence is here. And His victory lives within me now.

IT'S HERE

Certainly, Earth is a flawed place and there are many things that we will not yet completely experience until this world has passed and Heaven is fully here.

But until it's here in it's fullness, it's here in moments.

It's here when we ask God for His will to be done.

It's here when we unashamedly worship Him.

It's here when we fight for inclusiveness and unity.

It's here when we create and indulge in moments of authentic community.

It's here in the dinner parties.

It's here when we embrace and walk in the confidence that we are God's children— His kids that He loves and enjoys and roots on and is giving all of His inheritance to.

It's here when we have fun with God's other children.

It's here when we live with the knowledge that death has no power over us.

It's here when we live with the certainty that we are merely visitors to this earth and true citizens of Heaven. Our home isn't here. Our Home is better.

It's here when we stop worrying about the times but fix our eyes on the One who is the Beginning and the End.

It's here when we live as who we really are— a new creation, with a new purpose, and a new name.

God's victory is here and now— as we bring Heaven down to Earth.

With our actions. With our words. With our prayers. With our worship. With our identity found completely in who He is.

Hillsong Worship has a beautiful song called "As It Is (In Heaven)." The lyrics declare these truths so beautifully.

So I will sing like I will there
In the fearless light of glory
Where the darkness cannot find me
And Your face is all I see
Oh I will sing like a man
With no sickness in my body

Like no prison walls can hold me
I will sing like I am free
'Cause I know You love me
I know You found me
I know You saved me
And Your grace will never fail me
And while I'm waiting
Oh I'm not waiting
I know Heaven lives in me
I'll sing Holy, Holy
My heart, cries Holy
As it is, in Heaven
It is in me
We'll sing Holy, Holy
The earth, cries Holy
As it is, in Heaven
So let it be[20]

There is no need to wait.

As it is in Heaven, so let it be.

INTERRUPTED

As I'm typing this, I'm on a flight to Phoenix to see some of my dearest friends who have become like family, and to witness, mourn, and celebrate some big life moments alongside of them. I've been in a season of little sleep and working nonstop. I have deadlines piling up and have had many days of feeling defeated. I am racing to finish this book, and I have already flown six times this month for speaking engagements. Logic would say to miss the events happening this weekend, to not deter my focus from my workload, and to not allow any interruptions into my schedule.

But... Heaven.

We can't miss Heaven.

We must allow Heaven to interrupt us.

As I look out the plane window, I see a few full clouds scattered about, a flawless and deep blue ocean, and golden mountain ranges coming into view beside it. I couldn't be closer to what we think of *visually* when we think of heaven. But where I am flying couldn't be closer to what we can expect to *feel* like when we think of heaven. Once strangers, now family, coming together to feast and enjoy and celebrate God together.

We don't belong in a place of stress, doubt, loneliness, and fear.

Those are things of *this* world.

Let's remember the Home we are true citizens of.

Let's remember the new names we have already been given.

Let's remember the new creations we already are.

May heavenly things *constantly* interrupt our earthly things.

Every day of our lives...

May we practice Heaven.

QUESTIONS

In your own life, how can you better practice Heaven?

Think on worship, resting in God's presence, inclusion, and community. What are ways you can indulge in each of these things more frequently?

What are goals you currently have that are human-focused? What are goals that are Heaven-focused?

How would you and your community look differently if everyone was living "on Earth as it is in Heaven"?

ACTION

Think of a way to bring Heaven to Earth this week.

Perhaps it's planning a dinner party where you and your friends share about what God is doing in your lives.

Perhaps it's making time for a life-giving event you once felt you were too busy for.

Perhaps it's bringing someone with you to church this weekend.

Perhaps it's worshipping God in the morning before you go to work each day this week.

We don't want to miss His Kingdom, His will, and enjoying Him. Whatever it is for you, think of a way that you can practice Heaven better this week, and the habits you can create for the rest of your life.

God's victory is here when we bring His Kingdom to Earth.

GOD'S VICTORY IS HERE WHEN WE PRACTICE HEAVEN.

—
GOD'S VICTORY IS HERE AND NOW — AS WE BRING HEAVEN DOWN TO EARTH.

CHAPTER 14

THEY HAVE A NEW NAME

Let's get to the point.

Many people around us have been answering to some old names for far too long.

Let's just get to the point.

They do not need a book about those memories, past identities, or past names. They already know *those* far too well.

So let's get to the point.

We don't have the time and they don't have the time— they have wasted enough of their lives answering to their insecurities, answering to their fears, and answering to the limitations other people have put on them. They have wasted enough time settling for less.

They want more.

More joy.

More hope.

More purpose.

More confidence in who they are.

And isn't that the point?

Why *don't* they know who that is?

Certainly, **we can be the people** who tell them.

FOR EVERYONE

This new identity we have found in Christ is not just for us.

It's for everyone.

Now that we answer to a new name, we have a new life, and a new purpose. We are a part of something much bigger than our own story. We are a part of something vastly larger than our pasts and our old hurts— even larger than our old victories.

God's victory is here when we, the people next to us, the people on the other side of the world, the people we love, and the people we need to work harder to love— when we **all** answer to a new name.

We are a part of not just receiving, but also **speaking** the truths found in God's Word about His children. Since we know and have been changed by this saving Gospel, it is our responsibility and our greatest privilege to be so filled up by His truths that they are naturally pouring out of us to the world around us.

Are we speaking these truths to others? Or are we lying to them about their identities, making them feel less valuable than they are?

Are calling people by their true names? Or are we calling them by titles that tear them down and elevate our position and status to seem above them?

Are we being the mouthpieces of God to the world around us? Or are we being the mouthpieces of the world to God and His children?

When people we have spoken to make their works cited page, do our words line up with the words of God?

When the people around us look at their soundboards, are we a voice of truth they want to turn up?

Are we cutting into people's races, or are we running and fighting alongside them?

THE OTHER WARS

We are not the only rope being tugged and pulled in a tug o' war battle.

Everyone around us is a rope.

Every soul is being fought over.

Every person we come across—whether for a second, for a season, or for a lifetime—will be pulled one way or another by the way we speak to them and the way we treat them.

Which side of the rope will we tug on?

How will we use our feet to dig into the mud and stand for them? How will we use our hands to pull for them even while our fingers are bleeding? How will we call in other team members to join and fight alongside of us?

We are not the only war. We are also fighters in each other's.

Our words, our actions, our work ethic, our patience, our forgiveness, our compassion, and our love can help win the battle in someone else's life.

Ecclesiastes 4:12 says, **"A person standing alone can be attacked and defeated, but two can stand back-to-back and conquer. Three are even better, for a triple-braided cord is not easily broken."** (NLT)

We are not meant to do this life, this fight, alone.

God's victory is here when we fight for one another.

RESET, RESTORE, & REPRESENT

2 Corinthians 5:16-17 states:

"Because of all that God has done, we now have a new perspective. We used to show regard for people based on worldly standards and interests. No longer. We used to think of the Anointed the same way. No longer. Therefore, if anyone is united with the Anointed One, that person is a new creation. The old life is gone—and see—a new life has begun!" (VOICE)

Now that we have a new name, we have a new perspective on how we see others. Perhaps before we found our identity in Christ, we would struggle with comparison, competitiveness, or feelings of superiority over others. That earthy perspective is no longer. **Anyone** who chooses Jesus is a new creation. We must see His children through His perspective— as the new creations they truly are.

We must **reset** how we see God's people.

This passage continues...

"**All this comes from the God who settled the relationship between us and him, and then called us to settle our relationships with each other. God put the world square with himself through the Messiah, giving the world a fresh start by offering forgiveness of sins. God has given us the task of telling everyone what he is doing. We're Christ's representatives. God uses us to persuade men and women to drop their differences and enter into God's work of making things right between them. We're speaking for Christ himself now: Become friends with God; he's already a friend with you.**" (2 Corinthians 5:18-20 MSG)

Our relationship with Christ has been restored. Now it's time to restore our relationships with one another. This is where God's victory is, in the pursuit of reconciliation. Any division between us is a win for the Enemy. He loves children of God tearing apart other children of God. He loves the name-calling. He loves the hurtful words we throw at each other. He loves when we do his work for him.

God is calling us to crush the Enemy's battle plan and to fight back with truth. Speak truth to God's children. Speak truth to those who have hurt you. Speak truth to those who speak lies to you. You don't play by the same rules as the world— you're a completely new creation. You're on an entirely different team. While they are trying to fight for themselves, you are trying to fight for them too. They have a new name. And we have the opportunity to speak that to them. Every choice you make to speak truth, fight for someone else's identity, and reconcile a broken relationship is a choice for God's victory to reign on Earth as it is in Heaven.

We must set out to **restore** with God's people.

God has also given us the task of helping others restore their relationship with Him.

We are Christ's representatives.

What we say to the world, we say on His behalf. How we treat the world, we do on His behalf.

We must be careful that our words and our actions do not contradict His.

Throughout the Bible, Jesus is defined by love.

"Live a life filled with love, following the example of Christ. He loved us and offered himself as a sacrifice for us, a pleasing aroma to God." (Ephesians 5:2 NLT)

Throughout the Bible, God is defined by love.

"Beloved, let us love one another, for love is from God, and whoever loves has been born of God and knows God. Anyone who does not love does not know God, because God is love." (1 John 4:7-8 ESV)

As we set out to represent Christ and to reconcile others back to God, we may not always know exactly how to act, or precisely what to say, but we *are* told what the source of our motives ought to be. In 1 Corinthians 14:1, we are told, **"Let love be your highest goal!"** (NLT)

Representing Christ means being rooted and motivated by love.

1 Corinthians 13:4-7 tells us what that looks like. Perhaps we've heard or read these words, but they hold much more power when they are lived.

"Love is patient and kind. Love is not jealous or boastful or proud or rude. It does not demand its own way. It is not irritable, and it keeps no record of being wronged. It does not rejoice about injustice but rejoices whenever the truth wins out. Love never gives up, never loses faith, is always hopeful, and endures through every circumstance." (NLT)

Keeping in mind that we must do all things in love, before we do or say something—whether in person, in writing, online, or through any other form of communication—we can filter it through the Bible's description of love—

- By saying this, am I being patient?
- Is this kind?

- Am I saying this out of jealousy?
- Am I saying this to boast, show off, or out of pride?
- Is this rude to anyone?
- Is this demanding something to be my own way?
- Am I being irritable?
- Is this keeping a record of someone's wrongs?
- Am I rejoicing about injustice?
- Does this show endurance?
- Does this show faith?
- Does this show hope?
- Does this portray God's love as unending and unconditional?

The Scriptures have provided us with a practical filter through which to put our words and our actions, demonstrating to us how to live *a life filled with love* as Jesus did.

It's commonly said, "Don't judge a book by its cover." The truth is that at one point or another, we all do. We judge content by the packing wrapped around it. We judge products based on their reputation. We judge events based on other people's experiences.

So does the rest of the world.

And we are Jesus' book cover.

People will not want to know Christ if we aren't reflecting how loving He is.

People will not want to open His Book if we who are talking about it aren't enjoyable to be around.

People will not know the new name and the new identity they can have in Him if we don't properly represent a life made new by Him.

We are the packaging around the Word of God, we are the reputation Jesus has, and we are the example people are looking at to see if they want their own experience with Him.

We mirror the Hope they are looking for.

We must take that responsibility seriously.

We must reflect Him accurately.

We must **represent** His love.

That is our highest goal.

ALL OF OUR NAMES

The same names in the Bible that describe us, describe all of God's people—

They too are God's Friend.

They too are Chosen.

They too are God's Workmanship— specifically purposed and fashioned for good things.

God's Spirit lives inside of them; they too are His Temple.

They too are God's Plan A— His Messengers, His Ambassadors, and His Witnesses to the world.

They are Greatly Loved.

They are meant to enjoy life like God's Child.

They are completely Free.

They are entirely Brand New.

They too need patience in getting used to their new name.

They need the freedom to take off their masks and be who they really are.

They have the power to inspire others with their stories.

They too are a part of God's plan to have His Kingdom and His will on Earth as it is in Heaven.

God's deep desire is that we would tell the world about this new identity, speak these truths to the people around us, and demonstrate His love to all of His children so that they too can forget their old names and answer to new confidence, a new purpose, and a new name.

There is no time to waste.

God's victory is here— as **we** are made new.

God's victory is here— as **they** are made new.

God's victory is here— as we are victorious **together**.

QUESTIONS

What is a time in your life when you called someone by the wrong name—an identity that was not from the Word of God—and it affected them negatively?

What is a time in your life when you called someone by the right name—an identity that is from the Word of God—and it affected them positively?

What have you learned in your life about the power of words?

ACTION

Think on how you can reset, restore, and represent better in your life.

How can you reset how you think of some of the people around you?

How can you restore a broken relationship in your life?

How can you represent Jesus better to the world around you?

How can you, as someone with a new name, live your life more intentionally to help others discover theirs?

Think on these things and commit to a decision of action.

Act as if someone's identity depends on it.

Speak as if someone's perspective depends on it.

Fight as if someone's victory depends on it.

LET'S BE VICTORIOUS TOGETHER.

LET'S
BE
VICTORIOUS
TOGETHER

"As for me

My name is **Forgiven**

My name is **Free**

My name is **Brand New**

Loved, Wanted, Child of God, Created with a Purpose

And it's been a **pleasure** to meet you."

NOTES

---

1 - Strong, James. Strong's Exhaustive Concordance of the Bible. Abingdon Press, 1890. http://biblehub.com/greek/4053.htm

2 - Helps Word-studies, copyright 1987, 2011 by Helps Ministries, Inc. http://biblehub.com/greek/4352.htm

3 - Thayer, Joseph Henry. The New Thayer's Greek-English Lexicon of the New Testament, with Index. Lafayette: Book Publ., 1981. http://biblehub.com/greek/4053.htm.

4 - "Plagiarism." Def. 1. The Oxford English Dictionary. Oxford: Clarendon, 1961. en.oxforddictionaries.com/definition/plagiarism.

5 - This quote is attributed to Carl Jung.

6 - Bevere, Lisa. Without Rival: Embrace Your Identity and Purpose in an Age of Confusion and Comparison. Grand Rapids, MI: Revell, 2016. p. 181.

7 - Foster, Mike. People of the Second Chance: A Guide to Bringing Life-saving Love to the World. CO Springs, CO: WaterBrook, 2016. p. 8-9.

8 - This quote is attributed to Publilius Syrus.

9 - Smith, Judah. How's Your Soul?: Why Everything That Matters Starts with the inside You. Nashville: Nelson, an Imprint of Thomas Nelson, 2016. p. 24-25.

10 - Attridge, Harold W., et al. The HarperCollins Study Bible: New Revised Standard Version, including the Apocryphal/Deuterocanonical Books with Concordance. San Francisco: HarperSanFrancisco, 2006.

a – p.40
b – p. 53

11 - Ellicott, C. J. A New Testament Commentary for English Readers. London: Cassell, 1901. http://biblehub.com/commentaries/ellicott/genesis/32.htm.

12 - Furtick, Steven. "Just Call Me Jacob." Elevation Church. Matthews, NC. 20 July 2014. elevationchurch.org/sermons/just-call-me-jacob.

13 - Hillsong Worship. "What a Beautiful Name." Let There Be Light. Hillsong Music Australia, 2016.

14 - Elevation Worship. "Call Upon the Lord." Here as in Heaven. Essential Worship, 2016.

15 - Miller, Donald. Scary Close: Dropping the Act and Finding True Intimacy. Nashville: Nelson, 2015. eBook. p 19.

16 - Lewis, C. S. Mere Christianity. New York: HarperCollins, 2001. p. 134.

17 - Henry, Matthew. "Revelation 2:17." Matthew Henry's Commentary on the Whole Bible : Complete and Unabridged in One Volume. Peabody: Hendrickson, 1996. http://biblehub.com/commentaries/revelation/2-17.htm.

18 - Gill, John. An Exposition of the Revelation of S. John the Divine. London: Printed for George Keith, 1776. p. 30. Bible Study Tools. www.biblestudytools.com/commentaries/gills-exposition-of-the-bible/revelation-2-17.html.

19 - Wong, Daniel. "The Hidden Manna and the White Stone." Bibliotheca Sacra. 617th ed. Vol. 155. Dallas: Dallas Theological Seminary, 1998. Bible Study Tools. www.biblestudytools.com/commentaries/revelation/revelation-2/revelation-2-17.html.

20 - Hillsong Worship. "As It Is (In Heaven)." Let There Be Light. Hillsong Music Australia, 2016.

THANK YOU

Honestly, if I wrote out an entire thank you section, it would be a whole book all in itself.
I have teamed up with the best of them.
And this team isn't small.

So to all the amazing humans, gracious encouragers, and relentless warriors around this world who have fought for me and beside me— you know who you are. I couldn't have done it without you. Thanks for being my family, and thanks for being on my team.

I love being on yours.

ABOUT THE AUTHOR

―――

Hosanna Wong is a writer, speaker, and spoken word artist who shares stories of freedom and hope to various ages, cultures, and communities around the country. Known for sharing complex Biblical truths through simple, raw, and captivating stories and refreshingly accessible applications, Hosanna speaks and performs at churches, conferences, prisons, and various urban ministries year-round. Under the name Hosanna Poetry, she has released two spoken word albums and is the author of I Have a New Name and Superadded. A San Francisco native, Hosanna and her husband, Guy, are currently based in San Diego, CA.

ACCESS VIDEOS, BOOKS, ALBUMS, AND MORE
RESOURCES FROM HOSANNA, AND SEE WHEN
SHE IS SPEAKING AT AN EVENT NEAR YOU:
HOSANNAWONG.COM

FOLLOW ONLINE: